Tips, Tricks & Triumphs
from Member to Member

Handyman Club Library™

Handyman Club of America
Minneapolis, Minnesota

Tips, Tricks & Triumphs

from Member to Member

Credits

Mike Vail
Vice President, New Product & Business Development

Tom Carpenter
Director of Books & New Media Development

Mark Johanson
Book Products Development Manager
Handyman Club of America

Steve Anderson
Senior Editorial Assistant, Editor

Dan Cary
Photo Production Coordinator

Chris Marshall
Editorial Coordinator

Marti Naughton
Art Direction & Production

Jon Hegge
Photo Production & Photography

Dan Kennedy
Book Production Manager

Cover Photo

A clever masking trick made painting the trim on this new shed a snap for Henry Finn of Saint Paul, Minnesota (See page 49). Photo by Mark Macemon.

ISBN 1-58159-091-1

1 2 3 4 5 6/04 03 02 01

Handyman Club of America
12301 Whitewater Drive
Minnetonka, Minnesota 55343

www.handymanclub.com

Foreword

As the editor of *HANDY* magazine, I'm responsible for keeping our readers up-to-date on the newest and best methods, techniques and products in the fields of home improvement and woodworking. In this fast-paced, ever-changing DIY world, staying ahead of the pack can be quite a challenge. Fortunately, I have an endless supply of valuable information that's unavailable to editors of ordinary newsstand magazines. This vast reserve of handyman know-how is the members of the Handyman Club of America.

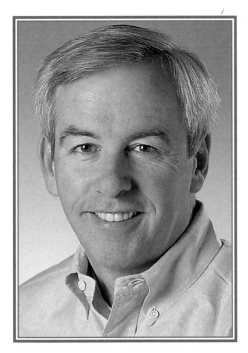

Since the Club's beginning, we've known that the best resource we have for doing DIY work more efficiently, with better results and for less money, is to rely on each other. Member input has always been an integral part of our philosophy and our success. *Tips, Tricks & Triumphs from Member to Member*, a book published exclusively by and for members of the Handyman Club of America, is both a testimony to our Club's success and a treasure trove of the hardworking wisdom that has gotten us where we are today.

Just as it's never easy to choose which submissions received by the magazine get featured in the HandyWorks and Tip Trader sections of *HANDY*, it was difficult to pare down the mountain of deserving mail to come up with the helpful hints and inspirational projects shown here. The tips in this collection were selected because they serve multiple purposes—not only will they help solve your home improvement or woodworking problems, they'll save you time and money in the process. In addition, we've chosen to feature more than 50 original furnishings, accessories and remodels that go beyond everyday published plans and reflect the builder's unique perspective.

I invite you to take a moment and thumb through this rich compilation. I'm confident that you'll discover a hint that will make your next task around the home or yard easier, or a project that will lure you back into the wood shop. Don't forget, it all comes courtesy of your fellow Club Members —the industry's greatest resource!

Tom Sweeney

Tom Sweeney
Executive Director
Handyman Club of America

Table of Contents

Member Tips

Member Projects

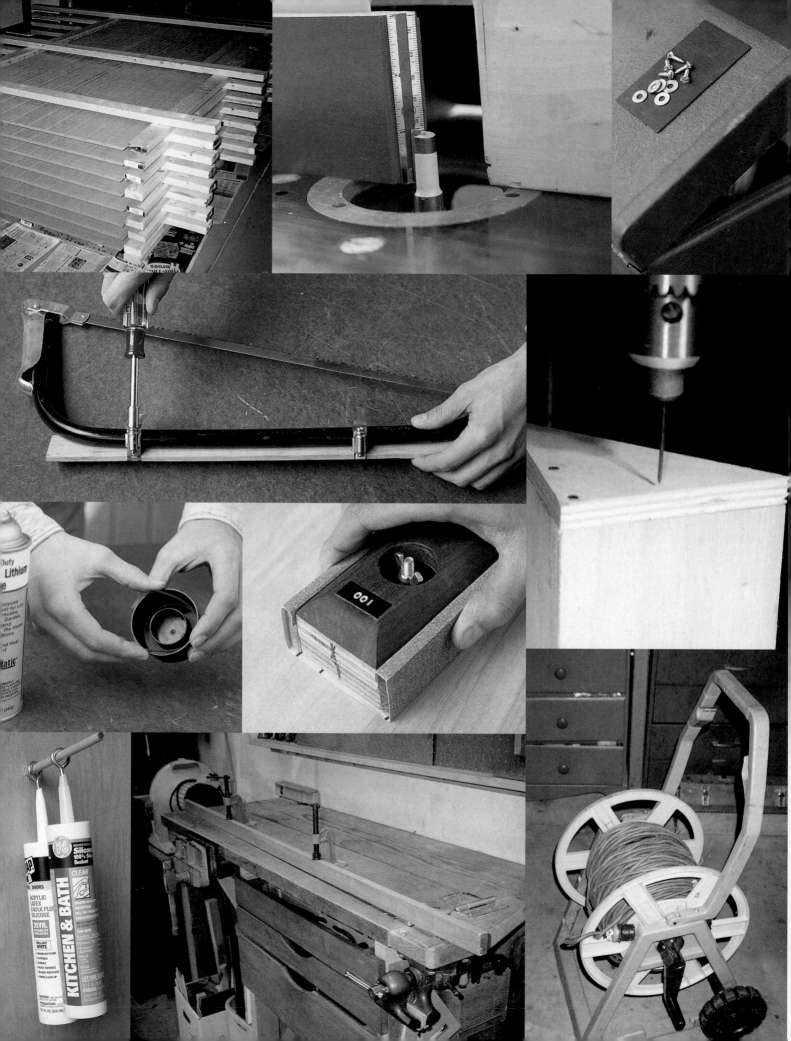

Member Tips

Handyman Club of America members exhibit unique problem-solving savvy when confronted with the hurdles of home improvement, woodworking and workshop tinkering. Whether it be devising time and money saving techniques, or discovering new uses for common tools and materials, what sets the handyman apart from the average do-it-yourselfer is a knack for thinking creatively. In the following pages, you'll find ample evidence that our members are truly resourceful in finding solutions. And you'll undoubtedly pick up a few good ideas to make your next project a shining success.

Handyman Tips

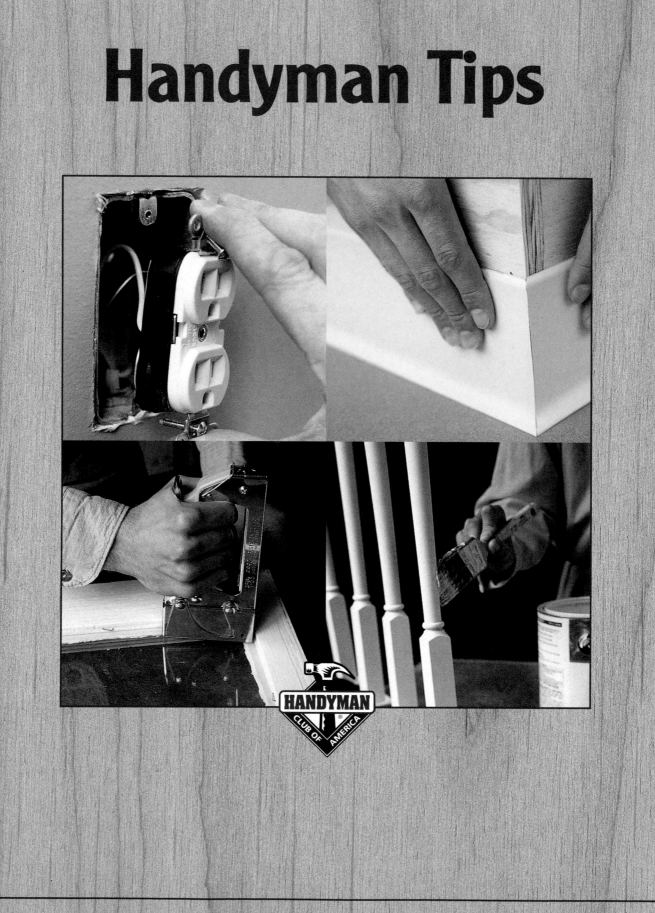

Keep an eye on your caulk

When I'm done using an unfinished tube of caulk, I insert a screw eye hook of the appropriate diameter into the tip. This is a great aid in restarting the caulk next time I need to use it. It also allows me to hang the tube over my workbench for use at a later date. When I unscrew the eye hook, the caulk flows freely every time.

David Schoepf
Marianna, Florida

Rack up your wintertime finishing projects

When I was building a backyard storage shed in the winter in Ohio, I was unable to topcoat outdoors in the freezing weather. So here's how I finished fourteen sheets of 4 × 8-ft. plywood siding in half of my two-car garage: I used the framing lumber stacked alternately to make a rack on which to apply the stain. The panels dried without any of the framing lumber touching the finished surface of the panels.

Dick Sellen
Westerville, Ohio

Install the pane in a pinch

Many of my projects use scrap material that I'm able to scrounge from various neighbors, which is one of the money-saving hints I've learned over the years. Although minor, the following tip is helpful at times when it isn't possible to go to the store. In the past, I've run out of glazier's points while replacing glass in a wood sash window pane. Rather than drive to the hardware store for more, I use my handheld staple gun. I hold it with the front end against the glass at an angle to the wood. I then release a staple part way into the wood and against the glass. Next, I apply glaze putty as usual. This little tip has helped me many times. I hope that it can help others as well.

Stuart Zimmermann
Hot Springs Village, Arkansas

A "tuck" pointer for running cable

During one of my weekend projects I wanted to relocate a small, inefficient lamp on the exterior left wall of the front entrance, to a more decorative matching pair of lamps on the front wall framing the entrance. Rewiring to the new location presented a problem. Surface conduit was out of the question due to aesthetic considerations. Drilling through the brick wall and rewiring from the inside was ruled out due to possible interior wall damage and the logistical matter of wiring the right side lamp to be located on the other side of the door from the electrical source.

After pondering the problem, I came up with a simple solution. I decided to bury the wire in the mortar joints of the brick wall. I used a diamond blade fitted to a grinder and was able to cut the channels in the mortar with little difficulty. Exterior ROMEX cable rated UF was used for added safety. After the cable was buried in the channel and the rerouting of the wire to the lamp on the right was accomplished by removing the molding above the door, I refilled the joint with more mortar. The entire project was performed in a weekend afternoon with excellent results.

Wayne Chin
Daly City, California

EDITOR'S NOTE: Local codes vary on how and where electrical cable can be run. Be sure to check the codes in your area before trying Wayne's tip at home.

Chalk one up for saving time

Here's a tip I use to save time while I chalk lines. First, punch a hole in the top and bottom of an empty film canister. Remove the hook from your chalk line. Thread the line through the bottom and top of the film canister, fill the canister with chalk, place the top on the canister and tie the hook back on the line. When you are chalking long lines (like stud walls on foundations), run the canister back and forth on the line instead of doing all that cranking and pulling the line out every time you need to rechalk. It even makes it easier to reel the line back in without getting the hook caught or tangled up.

Steven Bookless
Selma, California

Rubber hose holds threaded bolts in place

I keep several small pieces of rubber hose around my shop for better gripping on threaded rods and bolts (clear plastic tubing works, too). The hose prevents damage to the threads and holds the bolts in place so you can work on them (if you need to clamp them in pliers to grind the ends or make them shorter, for instance). If you try to hold them without the rubber hose, you'll probably lose your grip and spend a lot of time looking for your bolts.

Richard Drake
Greenfield, Indiana

Turning water into glue

Here in Minnesota I had to frame two houses in December. The ground was frozen, so there was no way to drive stakes to act as braces and keep the walls plumb. Since both houses had slab-on-grade cement floors, I took a gallon of water to work with me. I used some scrap lumber and froze the boards down to the floor about 10 ft. out from the sides (since they were 8-ft. side walls they didn't interfere with the building). Once the walls were raised I had a solid piece to nail the braces to. I kept the scraps frozen to the floor until the trusses were in place. It took a solid blow with a mallet to knock them loose.

Fred Doms
Boy River, Minnesota

"Paint Wheel" sends overspray away

Any spray painting I have to do must be done outside of my small shop, but there I'm at the mercy of the wind. So, to alleviate this problem, I sandwiched a 12-in. dia. lazy Susan bearing between two pieces of 5/8-in. CDX plywood to make a rotating paint platform that I could rest across a couple of sawhorses. This lets me keep my back to the wind as I spray.

The upper platform has a 36-in. diameter, whereas the lower platform has a 34-in. diameter. This keeps my fingers from getting caught between the two platforms as I spin the work around.

By keeping the "Paint Wheel" (as I call it) small and simple, I can store it easily on a wall or behind the shop hanging from a hook. Also, by not making it into a table, I can lay it on the ground when spray painting larger pieces such as rocking chairs. My grandchildren also like to use it as a twist board.

Simple but effective, the Paint Wheel can be used with either side up. And after several uses, it will look like a Picasso painting hanging on the wall of your shop or garage.

Bill Beatrice
Summerfield, Florida

EDITOR'S NOTE: Bill's clever "Paint Wheel" can also be used indoors (see photo, left) to allow you to apply an even coat of paint on larger projects, without walking around and around in circles while you spray.

Bungee cords at the ready

I'm always using bungee cords to secure one thing or another in the back of my pick-up truck. One day, I got tired of fighting to untangle the bungee cords in the toolbox of my truck, so I came up with this idea: securing them neatly on a piece of PVC pipe. I now save myself time and frustration with this simple, inexpensive fix. This has been a great idea for me, and I thought I would share it with my fellow club members.

Bill Morse
Rawlins, Wyoming

Tape measure marking gauge

Here's a tip I use a lot when marking insulation, insulating board and several other things. I've discovered that a quick and accurate way to measure is to "do it backwards." Here's how: With your regular tape measure, set your measurement and lock the tape in place. Then, run the housing part of the tape measure along the edge of whatever you're marking. Use the hooked end to mark the material. On foil-faced insulating board you can leave a mark right in the foil. With rolls of fiberglass insulation, just poke holes with the hooked end at two points along the line you want to cut, then grab your straightedge and slice it clean. This method is much faster than marking with a pencil. It also has less chance of getting a measurement wrong from cutting on the wrong side of your mark (especially on repeated and same length pieces). Although this is not a super accurate way to measure, for these applications it works great.

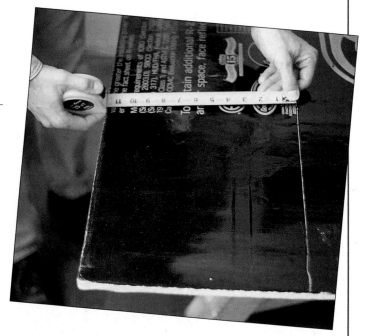

Rich Nahay
Meadville, Pennsylvania

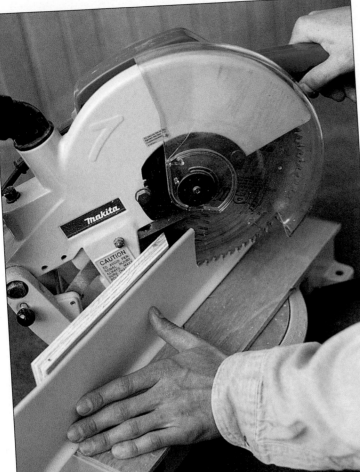

Miter jig helps cut baseboard smoothly

I found cutting vinyl baseboard difficult to do freehand. The flimsy vinyl kept flexing while I worked, and none of my cuts were straight. I needed better support while I cut. That's why I made this simple auxiliary fence that attaches to my power miter saw and acts as a backer board. Now, I'm able to make both angled and straight cuts quickly and accurately.

Nick Duzanica
Mountain View, California

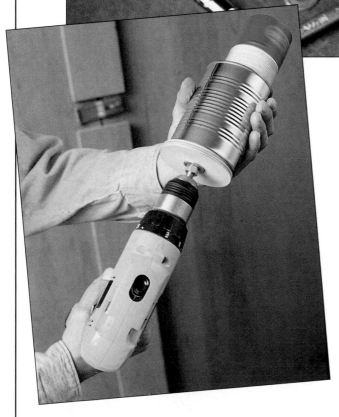

Let your drill do the mixing

Here's a tip for a better way to mix up 11-ounce cans of spray paint. I use a metal can (such as a soup can) that the paint can will fit inside of. I make a ¼-in. hole in the center through both the can and the disk, and install a ¼-in. bolt with the head inside the can. I then chuck the threaded end of the bolt in my drill and mix away. I have been using this method to mix spray paint for a year or more.

Chris Hagen, Jr.
Fairmont, Minnesota

Swivel tab

Getting a handle on sheet goods transport

Here is a simply constructed unit for easy carrying of 4 × 8-ft. panels by one person—with one hand. I cut the pieces for this jig and assembled it in just fifteen minutes. The swivel tab swings clear to allow the insertion of one or more panels resting on the lower block. Swing the tab back, tighten the wing nut and lift to shoulder height with the handle.

One ¾-in. panel or a combination of ¼ and ½-in. could be carried. Being 73 years old and no Arnold Schwarzenegger, one full ¾-in. plywood panel or one ½-in. drywall sheet is my limit. Of course, the unit could be modified to carry more.

Kermit Nordeen
Chesapeake, Ohio

Gain a foot from your claws

Have you ever needed to pound a nail a little higher than you can reach? Here's one way to do it with good results. First, wedge a nail backward between the claws of your bent-claw hammer, with the nailhead flat against the throat of the hammer head. Then, with a quick, sharp blow your nail will be set enough to drive it the rest of the way with just one hand. You can gain as much as a foot reaching with this technique.

Robert Develine
Delhi, California

Create a wire tunnel through your wall

Have you ever had to run thin electrical wire through a stud wall? It can be difficult to snake the flimsy wire in one side and out the other. After several frustrating attempts, I came up with a solution. Once the holes are drilled, I create a "tunnel" through the wall by running a drinking straw from one side of the wall to the other. I can run the light gauge wire through the straw and out the far side. No more headaches caused by a wire that won't go where I want it to.

R. Zimmerman
Farmington, New Mexico

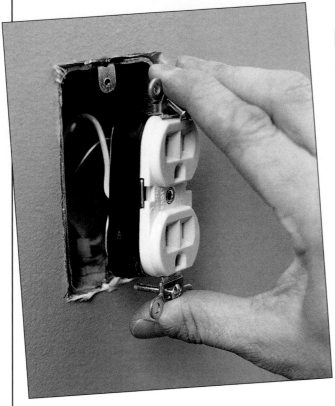

Electrical tape protects against shorts

I work for the maintenance department of the local school district. We used to have problems with receptacles shorting out against the sides of the metal boxes. The kids were constantly removing the screws or loosening them, causing the plug to short out. So, to correct the problem, I began to wrap the wall plugs and switches with electrical tape. This way, the screws would not come in contact with the metal box. We now do this with all new wall plugs and switches when they're installed. It may have stopped the fun the kids were having, but it sure helped those of us working in the maintenance department.

David DeFratus
Pottsboro, Texas

Cutting Plexiglas is a snap

The best way I have found to break Plexiglas is to use a hot woodburning iron with a thin blade and make a cut using a straightedge as a guide. This way, the Plexiglas breaks right off. The edges may be a little rough, so I use a putty knife or a scrap board to grind the cut area smooth.

Charles Haspel
Hilliard, Florida

Tape your file to protect your workpiece

As a maintenance person at a bible camp, I got the job of repairing a piano keyboard cover that was strained from being leaned on while something was under the lid. The hinges were screwed onto a strip of veneered flakeboard, and most of the screws in the hinges had been stripped.

In order to reset the screws in the soft flakeboard, I drilled a ¼-in. hole where each screw stripped out. I drilled the holes a little deeper than the lengths of the screws. Inserting a piece of ¼-in. dowel rod into the screwholes gave the screws a tougher material to bite into and created a better hold.

However, the dowel plugs were not exactly flush with the surface of the board. To make them flush I put tape on the two edges of the flat file, leaving a space between the tape pieces that was wider than the plugs. As I filed over the ends of the dowel rods, the teeth on the file cut away the excess without letting the teeth scratch the surface of the veneer. There was no marring on the varnished surface.

After I drilled pilot holes, the hinges were set and now the lid fits perfectly.

Paul Hartman
Taylorsville, North Carolina

Handy spindle painting technique

To paint cylinder-shaped workpieces such as spindles and balusters, I use this handy jig. It's nothing more than a line of screws drilled up through a scrap board. I clamp this board to my worksurface with the screw tips up. Then I drill holes (if they aren't already there) in one end of each of the workpieces. I stand the workpieces up with the help of the screws and then brush or spray on paint in a well-ventilated area. With the spindles held in place on the screws, I don't have to fight to rotate them. This is the easiest way I've found to consistently topcoat all the surfaces of my lathe-turned workpieces.

Louis Bernard
North Canton, Ohio

A better way to cope with molding

When coping a piece of molding, try using a spiral scroll saw blade in a jeweler's saw. The angle of attack is no longer a problem because the spiral teeth cut in any direction. Jeweler's saws are available at most building supply stores.

David Dunlop
Durmont, Colorado

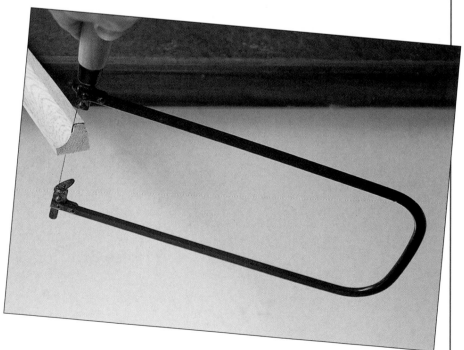

Lipstick marks the spot

When cutting outlet locations in drywall or paneling, I find it's helpful to use my wife's lipstick for marking. I color the edge of the electric box with the lipstick, then place it on the wall where the box will go. I press firmly to leave a print of the box, then I cut out the drywall or paneling along the lipstick lines. With this method, there's no guesswork or inaccurate measurements. I get perfect results every time!

Paul Russillo
Buffalo, New York

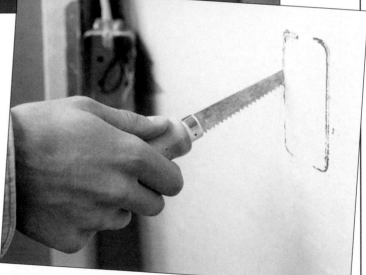

Workshop Tips

When space is tight, call in the vise squad

What's a guy to do when there's no room for a proper 8 or 10-ft. workbench? This is a problem rarely covered in DIY magazines.

We moved into a retirement community 2 years ago, and found very compact homes and even more compact garages. In fact, we found garages that barely hold two cars. I'm limited to a workspace 22 ½-in. wide × 15-ft. long.

Six of the 15 ft. are used for two metal double-door office-style cabinets, which I use for tools and general storage. The next 4 ft. are used for my band saw and disc sander stands (both on wheels). Some wall space is taken up by hand saws, pipe clamps and the like.

I'm left with only 4 ft. 9 in. of space for my workbench, so that's the size I built it. I knew it would be impossible to handle a decent project on such a small bench unless the top could be cleared of obstructions. For that reason, I have eight flush bolts for hold down clamps. But the basic problem was how to have a solid bench vise that could be cleared instantly out of the way.

The answer is shown above. It does everything I need it to do, and it was simple to make from parts available at my local hardware store. I used two hinges because there was a little looseness with only one, but with a pair there is absolutely no give in the hinge pins.

L. B. Fredericks
Mission Viejo, California

An idea that's sure to stick

To help keep small metal parts and fasteners from rolling around when I need them, I affix magnetic business cards or refrigerator magnets to a metal surface nearby (the top of my toolbox, for example). The loose parts will stick to the magnetic cards, making them easy to find whenever I need them.

Brock Whatley
Longview, Texas

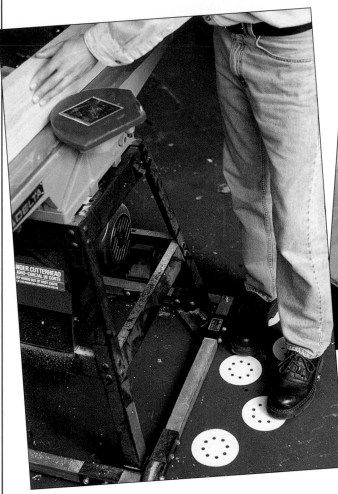

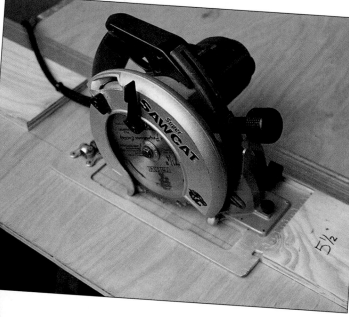

No more slippery shop floors

Slippery floors can be dangerous in workshops. For better traction on shop floors, I use stick-on sandpaper discs. I put these discs in front of certain machines where pushing is required, such as a table saw, a jointer or a table-mounted router. This is an inexpensive way to make your workshop safer.

David Stoltzfus
Bird-in-Hand, Pennsylvania

Scrap blocks set straightedge quickly

Here's a technique I use to place my straightedge quickly and accurately whenever I rip cut with my circular saw. I've cut scrap 1× blocks to the width of my saw's foot on either side of the blade. Now, instead of measuring each time from the cutting line to where I need to clamp the straightedge, I simply line the scrap spacer blocks up with the cutting line and place the straightedge accordingly. Then, I remove the scrap blocks and complete my cuts. I make two scrap blocks for each side of the saw's foot since the measurements are not the same, and the saw can be used to cut from either direction. Of course, you should always use correct safety measures such as eye and ear protection, and unplug the saw while measuring.

Stanley Smith
Wichita Falls, Texas

Soaking the rust away

Hand tools in the workshop that don't get used every day sometimes begin to show signs of rust. When this happens, I soak the tool in a non-corrosive container of inexpensive dark cider vinegar. For light rust, four hours should be long enough. For heavier rust, six to eight hours should do. When done soaking, wipe the tool with a scouring pad, rinse in warm water, dry and coat lightly with a rag dampened with oil. This method is easy and nearly always successful.

Gerry Scheuers
Keokeek, Iowa

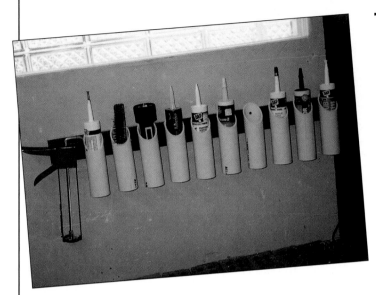

Totally tubular storage

Here's an easy project that I believe will help any handyman who's tired of having his caulk tubes rolling around his shop. I built this caulk tube rack out of 2-in. PVC pipe cut at a 45° angle every 8 in. The angle makes it easy to read the writing on the caulk tubes and lets me attach the PVC easily to a 1 × 4 on the wall. To keep the tubes from falling through the bottom, I simply drive a drywall screw through the tubes. These holders work great to store other similarly shaped items, such as flashlights, too.

Robert Martin
Latrobe, Pennsylvania

Ceiling-supported shelving

The walls of my shop are solid concrete reinforced with steel rods placed on 6-in. centers. (We laugh at hurricanes, and only a direct hit from a tornado will bother this place.) Needless to say, though, drilling holes for shelves can be a problem. So I opted instead to hang them from the rafters.

These hanging shelves are simple and quick to build, yet are extremely strong. They are made with 2 × 4 vertical supports and 2 × 6 horizontal shelves. I use mason jars with one-piece lids screwed to the bottom of each shelf with fender washers to keep the lids from turning.

The storage of assorted fasteners is within easy reach, and I've marked all four sides of each jar with its contents. As jars become available, (we can only eat so much spaghetti sauce), I install the newest jar alongside the others.

Bill Beatrice
Summerfield, Florida

Grind your rotary tool for more uses

To save time looking for a small screwdriver when it's time to change the cutting wheels on your rotary grinding tool, just grind down the rear of the wrench to form a flat tip that will fit tiny slotted screws.

Frank Doyle
Milford, Iowa

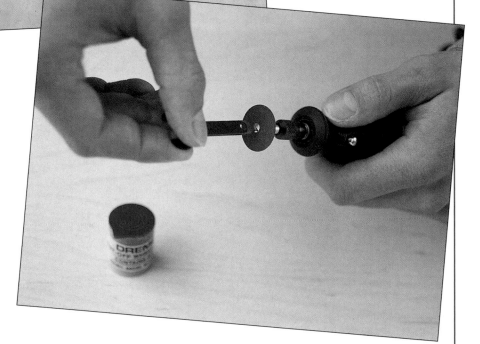

Handy pick-up tip

These gadgets have helped me pick up dropped screws, nails, small wrenches etc. off the floor in my shop, and while working outdoors as well. To make them, I use the centers from old stereo speakers, which are magnetic. They have a hole in the center, which helps to mount them. I use epoxy to glue a small speaker magnet onto a straight pipe for use in the shop. For outside, I put a larger speaker magnet on wheels, which is great for use after a roof job or any other construction project where nail pick-up is an issue. I've made a couple of these for friends, and they also found them quite convenient for various jobs.

Chester Harvey
Des Moines, Iowa

Taking charge of batteries

What to do with all those awkward battery chargers? If you set them on your worktable, you're not left with much space to work on. If you put them in your cabinet, oftentimes there's not enough clearance to charge them, or you can't run a power cord to them. To solve this dilemma, I mount a piece of pegboard on a wall above my work area. I hang the chargers on hooks and run a cord to an outlet strip. This way, the battery is charging and I can work on my tabletop.

Bruce Pennington
Chesapeake, Virginia

Wrap your paint cans for freshness

Here's a tip I've used for years now to solve the problem of partial gallons of leftover paint drying up. When I lived in an apartment years ago, I used to keep paint on hand for repairs. It seemed like a good idea, until it came time to use it. Every time I opened the cans, I found a thick skin of dried paint, making it impossible to mix so it would match. After trying several different methods for preserving the paint, I discovered one that I really like.

Here's the tip: Before closing the can, I place a regular plastic shopping bag over it, pushing the bottom of the bag into the can until it rests on the surface of the paint. Then I press the sides of the bag against the side of the can, overlapping the top of the bag to the outside of the can. The bag covers the grooves for the lid, making a tight seal. Replace the lid as usual, trim the excess bag if you wish and store the paint. I have stored paint for two years and found it in great condition using this technique.

Paul Loftin
Claremont, North Carolina

A jewel of a blade storage solution

I've found that plastic CD jewel cases are great for storing my 3⅜-in. and 4½-in. trim saw blades. These blade holders will also fit in your toolbox.

William Pindar
New Paltz, New York

Hidden horse saves space in workshop

Because of a small shop, I built this "space-less sawhorse" to attach to my workbench. It's always on the job and never in the way. I used two scrap hardwood 2 × 6s and one 1 × 6 (mine were 32 in. long, but this varies depending on the length of your workbench). This handy addition also serves as an extra table when I put a piece of plywood on top of it.

Neil Everts
New London, Wisconsin

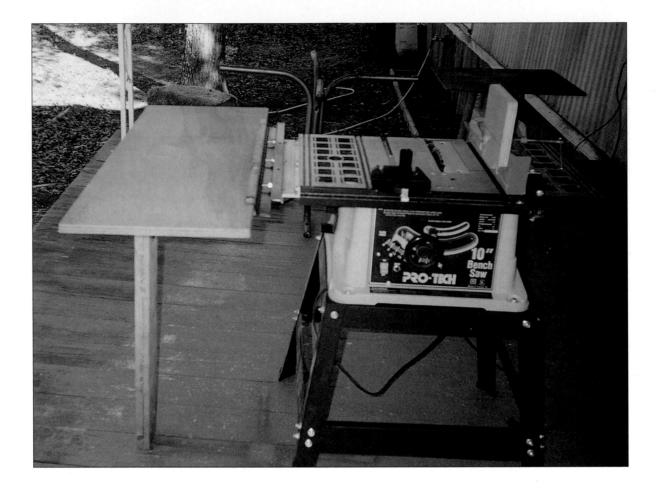

A thoughtful table extension

This benchtop table jig is my own invention made out of old scraps that I had around my shop. The idea came to me one day when I needed to cut a larger piece of stock. I needed an extra extension because the table of the saw just wasn't large enough by itself. So I started hunting for some material that would work as an auxiliary table. I eventually found a plywood scrap and two aluminum L-brackets. I drilled holes in the aluminum to match those already in the saw table. I then used another piece of aluminum to bolt to the swinging furniture hinge, thereby connecting all the pieces together. It really took me a long time to figure out how to get this frame to work. I also had to countersink the holes in the top of the frame and use flathead wood screws as fasteners so the work would slide across without hitting the screws. Although there are many different ways to brace the table, I just used the simplest. This jig was a lot of hard "thinking" work, but it paid off.

Freddie Garvin, Jr.
Vernon, Alabama

Keep straws under your cap

Here is a tip for those of us handymen and women who tend to lose the precision spray straws that come with some lubricating sprays and cleaners. If you're like me and like to put the cap back on the product after using lit, but hate having to tape the straw on the side of the container, here's the solution: Before you put the cap back on the can, slip the precision straw into the outer cup on the inside of the cap. The straw will bend around the shape of the cap and store neatly away when not in use. It may be bent slightly, but at least you'll know where to find it.

Albert Rodriguez, Jr.
Grandview, Washington

Roll, roll, roll your cord

If you need to use long extension cords, but can't seem to keep them from tangling up all the time, here's the solution: Use an old garden hose reel! Mount a spring clip on the inside (near the bottom) to hold the male plug. Wind the cord onto the reel, ending with the female plug. Tie-off or mount a second spring clip to the outside. When you go to use the cord, set the reel next to the receptacle, pull the cord and the female end toward where you are working. Return the cord to the reel once you have finished.

Bruce Pennington
Chesapeake, Virginia

Woodworking Tips

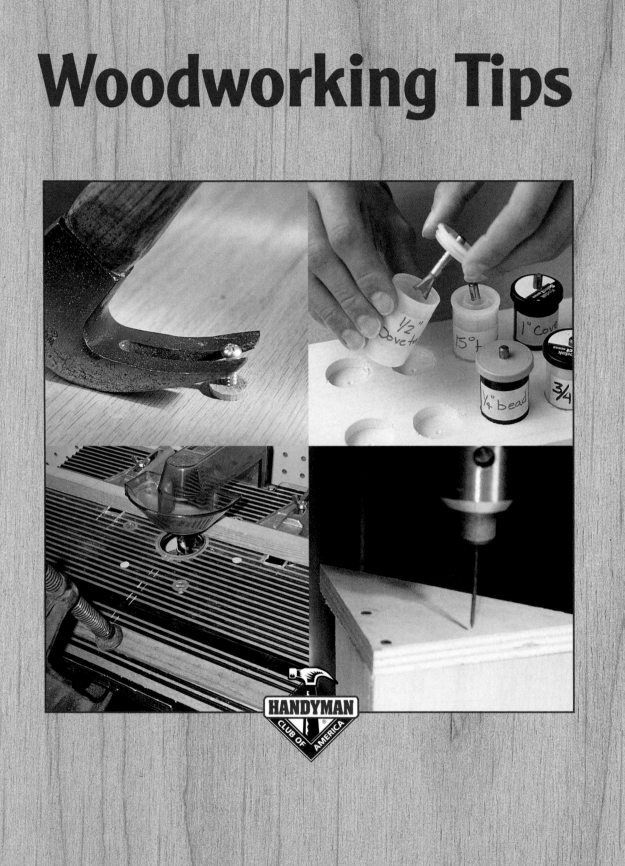

A grit off the old block

I created this handy little sanding block design because of all the hand sanding I do in my wood shop. I made one for each type of grit, which makes it easy to locate the correct grit for each particular job.

Bob Pflieger
Albuquerque, New Mexico

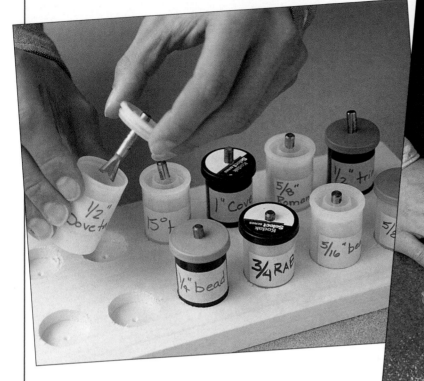

Recycling old film canisters, bit by bit

I use plastic snap containers that hold 35-mm film to store my router bits. I drill a ¼-in. hole in the lid, place the bit in the container and then replace the lid, allowing the shank of the bit to protrude through the ¼-in. hole. I place masking tape around the container and label it with the size and style of bit contained within. These plastic containers protect the bits from nicks and rust, and allow them to be easily stored and identified in a toolbox or cabinet. In my shop, I use scrap lumber to create a base that holds all my router bit containers. These film canisters can be obtained at no charge from any one-hour photo mart or local camera store. They also make great storage containers for razor blades or other small cutting devices.

Charles Stansbury
Olympia, Washington

A honey of a hint

When you're working in your shop or on your bench, sawdust and wood chips gather in cracks and in crevices on your workpiece and elsewhere. Instead of blowing them out with your mouth and getting sawdust in you eyes and face, just use an empty honey container with a ¼-in. extension tube taped to the end. This is a safe method to clear away dust and particles while you work. I've found that the honey bottle blower is a very handy thing to have around my wood shop.

Philip Meloche
Tuscon, Arizona

Groovy router table goes the way of disco

My router table is grooved on the top and, as many members well know, soft white pine can get marred when being pushed over this surface. To solve this problem, I have cut an ⅛-in. piece of Plexiglas for the top and locked it down with a C-clamp in front and the router table guides in the back. I have cut out a circle in the Plexiglas for the bit to stick through. Now, my routed pine work-pieces are always free of unsightly grooves. This sure has cut down on the amount of time I need to sand out the table marks.

Gerald Allen
Louisville, Kentucky

Labels save time in the wood shop

Here's how to find lumber fast in your wood shop: I save time looking for the right piece of wood by marking the size and species near the end of each board. You can also write any special charac-teristics such as burl or curly grained. This is a real timesaving tip when you're looking for one specific piece for a particular use.

Sarah Davis
Bluefield, Virginia

Wax your teeth

For over 40 years, I have used paraffin wax to protect and lubricate my saws and planes. Not only does this technique protect the tools from rust, it also makes for easier cutting. A bar of paraffin wax is inexpensive and lasts much longer than spray lubricants, plus there is no sticky residue left behind or cans to roll around in the shop. A piece of paraffin wax needs little space, and can be carried in a pocket, a nail apron or a toolbox.

Robert Grant
Tucumcari, New Mexico

Sticking it to your sander

To keep sandpaper from ripping out at the clamps on each end of a palm sander before the sandpaper is worn out, I stick a strip of 1 × 1-in. double-sided tape to the palm sander pad. This will secure the sandpaper to the pad so that the paper will not tear due to the 180° bend it must make to be clamped.

Ashley Greer
Paris, Texas

Sandpaper on a stick

Here's a sanding tip I have used for years: I take a ⅜ or ½-in. dowel that's 5-in. long and cut a slit down the middle with either a hack saw or a band saw. I then cut a piece of sandpaper 1-in. wide × 2-in. long. I insert the sandpaper into the slot and wind it counterclockwise. I use this homemade detail sanding stick in my drill press to finish-sand some of my scroll saw work. When the sandpaper wears out, I just cut a new strip—quick, easy and inexpensive!

Al Zantjer
Gobles, Michigan

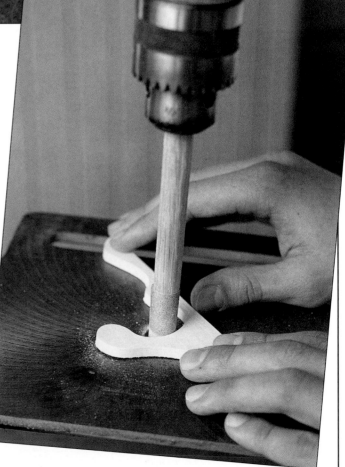

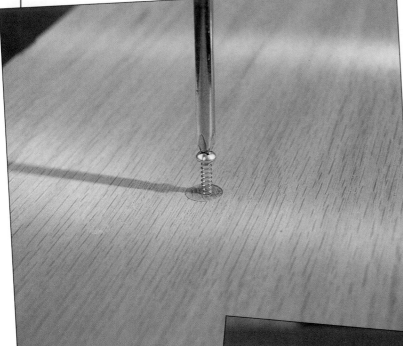

Unplugging screwholes

If you need to take something apart that is held together by countersunk screws covered with flush plugs, here's how to do it: First, twist a small screw part way into the wood plug. Then pull the plug out carefully with a claw hammer. You may need to clean out the screwhole with a chisel if some of the plug sticks. Now the screwhead should be exposed and can be easily removed.

David Stoltzfus
Bird-in-Hand, Pennsylvania

Gauging every bit

Here's a quick and easy gauge I built for setting the bit depth and fence location on my router table. I cut a 45° bevel on one end of a scrap piece of plywood and attached an old measuring gauge to the bevel cut. This device reads the elevation of the router bit when held vertically, and, when held perpendicularly to the fence, this gauge accurately measures the distance between the bit and the fence. It can be difficult to use a rule to determine these distances due to the cut-outs on some router table fences.

Sarah Davis
Bluefield, Virginia

Precision nail driving on the drill press

Did you know that if you own a drill press you could use it as a nail driver? Simply add a cylinder magnet (such as those popularly found attached to a telescoping rod handle) to your drill press chuck and you'll discover a whole new world of accuracy and precision by hand-feeding nails to the magnet individually and lowering the quill handle as a driver. I suggest using the "box nails" with flat heads, as they will provide the best overall results.

Phil Duck
Columbia, South Carolina

Home & Yard Tips

Molding brings limbs within reach

January 2000 brought with it some of the heaviest snow storm conditions to South Carolina in over 100 years. It brought down numerous tree limbs throughout my front yard. One particular branch was left dangling over the front walkway from about 20 ft. up. I didn't want to pay the exorbitant fee to have a tree removal company finish bringing it down. I knew I had a 14-ft. stick of rigid oak molding in my garage. I then came up with a simple solution by using two stainless steel radiator hose band clamps to attach my tree limb hand saw to the end of the molding. This extension saw was sufficiently long and sturdy to allow me to trim the branch safely from the sidewalk. It was amazing how this new tool cut.

Phil Duck
Columbia, South Carolina

No-slip trash can liner

Here's a surefire way to keep garbage can bags from falling into the can. First, take a new or used heater hose or garden hose and cut it to the length of the can's circumference. Use a utility knife to split one side of the hose the full length. Put the bag in the can as usual. Slip the hose over the lip of the can with the liner beneath it. The bag is held in place until it's time to take out the trash.

Carl Creech
Mountain Home, Arkansas

Another option for holding bags in place

My favorite tip is a quick and easy way to keep the trash bag liner from falling into the garbage can once trash is deposited. This simple trick consists of a large rubber band connecting a piece of heavy-duty string that can be slipped over both the bag and the rim of the can. I tie about a 1½-yd. length of string to the rubber band. The string will stretch over the top of the can and hold the bag firmly in place.

Roy Knight
Avondale, Georgia

Heat keeps plaster intact

When hanging a picture on a plaster wall, heat the hanging nail with a flame before driving it into the wall. This way, the nail enters the wall with less resistance. As a result, you won't crack or chip the plaster when you tap it home.

Arthur Elson
Troy, Ohio

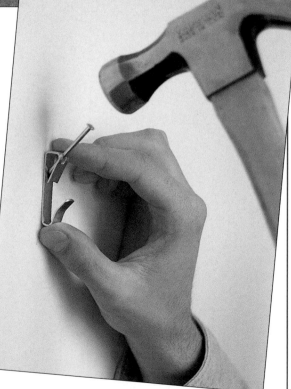

Don't get "leafed" behind when using your shredder

Here's my tip for more efficient operation of a medium-size leaf shredder. Although my shredder/chipper works fine, the back that came with it is too small to pick up a lot of leaves. It kept me busy emptying and reattaching it. Starting and stopping the engine so frequently was a nuisance. To solve the problem, I fastened the end of an old lawnmower bag onto a short length of stovepipe and attached the other end of the cut-off bag to the shredder's leaf exhaust port with wire hooks. These hooks are detachable so the stovepipe can be removed for storage.

Next, I turn my yard waste cart on its side and put the cover I made for the top opening of the cart in place. Half of the covering is wood and half is screen wire. I cut a hole in the wood in which to slip the stovepipe. I fasten the cover to the cart with two ropes and a slipknot. If the cover is not fitting tightly and some ground leaves fly out, I just drape an old bedspread over the spaces. When the cart is full of ground leaves, I loosen the ropes, turn the cart upright and roll it to where I want to dump the leaves.

I. J. Miller
Winston-Salem, North Carolina

Masking trimwork the waxed-paper way

Here's a foolproof technique for painting or staining new trimwork without masking with tape or careful cutting-in. Before you install the trim, tape some waxed paper to the wall where the trim is being attached. Then attach the trim. Now you can slop on the paint or stain as fast as you wish without getting any on the walls. When the paint is dry, just pull out the waxed paper. I used this technique when painting the trim on my new shed and it worked great.

Henry Finn
Saint Paul, Minnesota

How to mask trimwork with waxed paper

1 Tape strips of waxed paper over the wall surface in the area where the new trim is to be installed (the case molding on the head of a shed door is shown here). Be sure to keep tape out of the installation area itself.

2 Attach the trim molding permanently, then paint it. The waxed paper will mask the wall surface from the paint, so you don't have to be overly careful (but don't get too sloppy either: too much excess paint will run off the waxed paper and make a mess).

3 Remove the exposed wax paper. In some cases, it will tear easily or even slip out. But you may need to trim it flush to the molding with a utility knife.

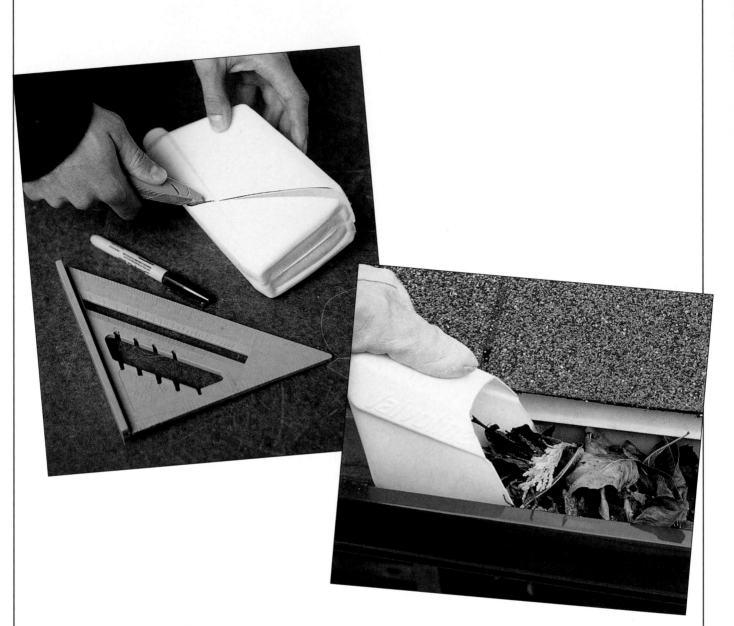

Homemade scoop leaves nothing in the gutter

I cut a 45° angle onto an empty, quart-size plastic oil bottle to use as a scoop when removing dead leaves from gutters. This size bottle will fit almost any size gutters.

William Joudrey
Casselberry, Florida

Under-counter sealing

Many kitchen countertops are made of particleboard, which is basically just glue and sawdust. A water-resistant surface, such as ceramic tile or laminate, is added to the top. Particleboard by itself will absorb water and begin to expand and fall apart. While most people protect against water damage on the top of the counter, they fail to watch out for it under the edges of the counter.

Dishwashers can leak steam and moisture from around their gaskets. Water can also run around the edge of the countertop just enough to get to the particleboard. This damage could lead to an expensive countertop replacement.

An easy way to prevent moisture from reaching particleboard is to spread a coat of silicone caulk over these areas. It won't be visible and it will resist water for many years. Don't wait until it's too late. Do it before trouble shows up!

Everett Smith
Ludington, Michigan

Something fishy about weed-eater line

While trying to install an underground telephone line from my house to my workshop, I had a problem getting the telephone cable through the electrical PVC pipe because the cable came folded in a package. I did not have a steel fish tape on hand, so I looked around to see what else I could use. I noticed my row of weed-eater line and gave it a try. It pushed through the pipe with the greatest of ease. I taped the end of the telephone wire to the weed-eater line and pulled it through. Who needs a steel fish tape when you have weed-eater line?

Al Schoppe
Temple, Texas

Getting an aspirin-free grip on your pane

Sometimes something as simple as replacing a broken window-pane can be a little unwieldy. I've discovered a simple solution for this problem. I make tabs of folded tape and attach them to the replacement pane. This gives my fingers something to take hold of while I set the glass into position. It can be almost any kind of tape, so long as it can support the weight of the pane I am replacing. This tip really makes an oftentimes annoying task a lot simpler!

Phil Duck
Columbia, South Carolina

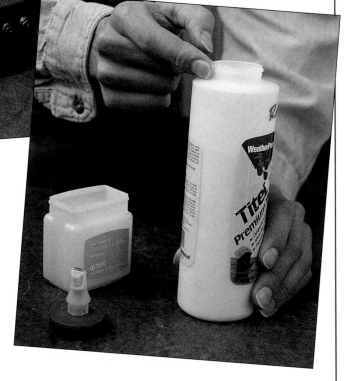

Soap bottle oil change during chainsaw pit stops

Refilling chain saw oil can be easier using a recycled dish soap container. Eliminated are the carrying of funnels and other cumbersome containers, which are replaced by small, pocket-size bottles providing a squirt whenever it's needed in the reservoir. A spare dish soap bottle fits in most large jacket pockets, keeping a hand free for carrying the saw and the fuel.

Gil Raynor
Brentwood, New York

Glue lids unstuck

If you find that the tops are sticking to your bottles of glue, try rubbing a little petroleum jelly around the rim. This tip works on paint cans, too.

Arthur Elson
Troy, Ohio

Get a church key for pocket change

I hate having to hunt for tools just to get a project started. One of the things I'm always misplacing is the church key to open paint cans. When I got tired of hunting for this elusive tool, I discovered that pocket change works great for opening a can of paint (quarters work the best). Place the quarter where you would a church key and start working the lid off as you go around. Although many people just use a screwdriver, you risk ruining the tip of the tool and kinking the lid of the can so it won't reseal properly. This is an easy solution that uses something most people already have in their pockets anyway.

Sterling Rachwal
Winnebago, Wisconsin

Painting the impossible

I have been painting houses for 18 years. A few years back, I discovered this handy tip by mistake, and have kept it under my belt until now. It's probably my best-kept secret. Here it is: Has painting over silicone ever been a problem? You say it can't be done? Try brushing some sanding sealer on the silicone first, let it dry, then topcoat with any paint you desire. This method will bond all paints, both interior and exterior.

Jerry Smitson
Tell City, Indiana

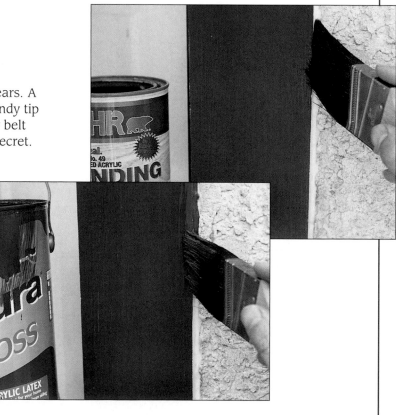

Concrete patching method is rock solid

I have a wonderful tip for filling holes or cracks in concrete blocks. I have been using this trick for over eight years. First, I mix auto body filler with a white hardener. I use this color instead of red so the filler will better match the concrete. I fill the hole with this mixture and then smooth it out. You can add additional coats as needed. It dries within 15 minutes. The area is then ready for painting.

Mark Wells
Grove City, Ohio

Fillet-O-Foam

As an automobile upholsterer for more than a half-century, I was always having problems cutting thick foam to an accurate size and shape. I had used hack saw blades and various other methods of cutting, but they were never satisfactory. My wife had an electric carving/fillet knife that she never used, so I decided would try cutting foam with it. Now, I am on my third knife! The blade will cut upholstery material up to 4-in. thick.

E.W. McKibben
Birmingham, Alabama

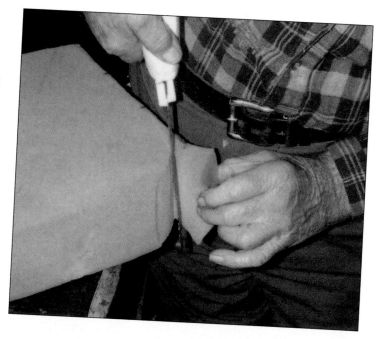

Member Projects

Nothing satisfies a true handyman like a job well done. After the last screw is driven or the final topcoat applied, then comes the real reward—the chance to step back and admire all of our hard work. But in the Handyman Club of America, we think others should be able to admire our work as well. The following pages feature a wide range of original designs that display both the creative talents and building proficiency of your fellow Club Members. From furniture-making to remodeling, the projects here are sure to impress and inspire.

Furniture

Custom case means no more "wining" for bottle storage

Here's a wine case project I started after a neighbor and long-time friend of mine saw a clock kit I assembled for my son's wedding gift. She liked the workmanship and commissioned me to build this large wine case for use in a restaurant she was opening. I had built smaller things over the years, and figured this would be a good challenge. Little did I know it would take 750 hours and five months to complete!

The only requirements were that the case had to hold at least 50 bottles for display, and it had to be sized for later use in a home with a standard 8-ft. ceiling. I began the design process by drawing the case with the help of my CAD software. I am a retired engineer, and the CAD work brought back memories of my active engineering days. The CAD software also provided me with full-scale templates for sawing the curved pieces. The overall dimensions of the cabinet are 86¼H × 41½W × 16D. The 215-pound completed case consists of three major sections to facilitate moving. They are: the top crown, the rack/display area holding 56 bottles, and the lower storage area that can accommodate 100 bottles.

Unique features include an inlaid ceramic plaque with a hand-painted magnolia (the Mississippi state flower), which ties into the décor of the restaurant. There are keyed locks on the left-side doors only, but I added keyholes in the right-side doors for symmetry. Antique-finished brass wire mesh fronts all the doors, which allows for viewing of the displayed bottles in the middle cabinet. Inlaid embossed panels centered behind the mesh in the bottom plywood doors help conceal the storage cavity and its contents.

The wine case is crafted of red oak. The finish is natural, with a few sprayed-on coats of semi-gloss varnish. To achieve a totally smooth surface, I wet sanded with 1200 grit paper, followed by #0000 steel wool, and finally a FFFF

grit pumice stone. The finished case then had a final paste wax applied to it.

It's worth reviewing a valuable lesson I learned from building this wine case. It's vital to know the scope of your project. I initially thought the project would take only a couple of months, but that was underestimating. Since I had no router experience, there was also a learning curve built in to the wine case.

Martin Fagot
Bay St. Louis, Mississippi

Deceptively roomy desk

Here's one of my favorite woodworking projects. I made this custom computer desk for our home office. I proportioned the desk so it's big enough to hold the keyboard and speakers for the computer. To get the desired desk width of 24 in., I edge-glued two pieces of 1 × 12-in. stock and used dowel pins to reinforce the joints. On the right side of the desk is a door that I made to look like three vertical drawer faces. The door opens to a cabinet that houses our CPU. The top shelf above the writing surface forms an "L" shape that holds the scanner, monitor and printer. This shelf is held up by three spindles that I turned on my lathe.

Everett Blehm
Sweet Home, Oregon

Kitchen nook isn't just for breakfast anymore

For her kitchen, my daughter wanted a table and bench that would take up less room than chairs and a table. To meet her needs, I made this oak corner nook. I added a mitten box/seat to help keep winter items handy and make it easier to dress her three boys for play outside in the snow. She wanted the piece to be durable because, well, boys will be boys.

To make the corner, the seat angle is cut at 22½° on both sides, and the back is a compound miter cut 7° × 22½°. I made the legs a little wider to cut out around the baseboard, and dressed up the top with a 3-in. board so that the bench could butt up against the wall and hide the baseboard heating. The mitten box is attached to the back with screws that are driven underneath so they don't show. This unit gives plenty of storage for hats and mittens. It has a child-safe hinge that holds it open to avoid injury. The table is a trestle design. I used mortise and tenons to hold the trestle legs in place. There is an oak stretcher between the legs.

Robert Lopes
North Dighton, Massachusetts

Handcarving replicates bygone style

I made this cherry display cabinet to resemble the old French "Art Nouveau" style of furnituremaking. All the wood is solid Pennsylvania cherry. The project includes lots of handcarved details throughout.

Dave Peterson
Calumet, Michigan

Custom cabinet determines what's in store

I constructed this cabinet for my wife, who needed extra shelves to display pieces of our pitcher and creamer collection. We searched many stores in our area, but could not find the proper size, style or finish to suit our needs. In order to get what we wanted, I decided to make it myself.

The construction material is 100% oak. Dimensions, in inches, are 32H × 36W × 7D. The shelves are adjustable and the back is made of oak wainscoting fastened only at the edges so the panel can float with the expansion of the wood. Gallery rails were handmade, and it is faced with rope moldings. I finished it with golden oak stain and multiple coats of satin polyurethane.

John Lezousky
Schnecksville, Pennsylvania

Championship bunk beds

I have a six-year-old son, Rob, and a four-year-old, Pete. Rob was getting an unbelievable amount of homework in first grade, so I wanted to build him a desk where he could do his schoolwork. Once I began planning the project, I decided to remodel the whole room into something functional, yet fun. Since both kids like to sleep in the same room, I needed two beds. I also thought it would be cool to have the desk incorporated into the beds somehow.

The top bunk is made of 2 × 10s supported by 4 × 4 posts, along with 2 × 4s ripped in half for the ladders and rail. These are held together by ⅜-in. carriage bolts. The headboard is made of 2 × 8s, and some plastic finials finish off the foot. The desk has a three-drawer cabinet underneath a 32-in. solid-core door for the top. The door was on the seconds rack at the lumberyard, and the pre-drilled hole for the doorknob was cut out so the 4 × 4 from the bed could pass through it.

There's a fluorescent light under the bed to illuminate the desktop, and there are some shelves built into the wall behind the head of the bed. I put one of the existing beds perpendicular to the top bunk underneath, and finished off the room by painting huge sports pictures on the walls and adding a soccer ball ceiling fan and light. The kids just love their new room!

Mike Schrader
Berlin, Wisconsin

The right angle isn't always 90°

We live in an octagon-shaped house that doesn't have a lot of storage. To help solve this problem, I looked around the house to see where I could put a corner storage unit. Once I found a suitable corner, I measured to see how big I could make the built-in cabinet without interfering with the bracket that ties the curtain back. The idea was to get the maximum amount of storage. Although I could have made the piece for display purposes (with glass doors, a mirrored back, etc.), my wife just wanted a place to store miscellaneous items. That's why I made it with solid doors. This corner cabinet project was part of my wife's honey-do list, and she is a honey.

David Smith
Harrison, Arkansas

Twin units lend a hand in the kitchen

I built this microwave cart (photo right) from oak in the Shaker style. The two drawers that give the illusion of being four drawers were made using a dado around the outside and down the center to resemble raised panels on each side. I put round decorative drawer knobs on each panel, which adds to the four-drawer effect. Behind the two raised panel doors is a sliding shelf centered top to bottom. I left the back of the microwave hutch open for ventilation. There's a small stopblock across the back to keep the microwave in place. The oak water cooler stand (photo left) was also made for my kitchen. It has one drawer and an adjustable shelf used to store paper cups and other items.

Robert Lopes
North Dighton, Massachusetts

Straight from the gossip mill

Since my retirement in 1998, I've been woodworking in my shop at home. This gossip bench, which I recently finished making for friends of ours, is one of my favorite projects. The bench needed to serve multiple purposes for its new owners. It had to hold both the telephone and the telephone books. It also needed storage space below the bench. This design meets all those requirements. Below the sitting area I mounted two doors with concealed European-style hinges. The handle on the drawer below the telephone shelf is made from oak shaped with a belt sander and attached with a screw from inside the drawer face. After staining and brushing on a few coats of polyurethane, I hand-rubbed four coats of paste finishing wax. The new owners love their bench and I'm pleased with my original design.

Everett Blehm
Sweet Home, Oregon

Bench of a higher order

This is my own design for a deacon's bench. I've made versions of this bench out of both oak and walnut. The overall measurements (in inches) are 31H × 36L × 19W. The seat opens to provide hidden storage space.

Bennie Pospisil
Mount Vernon, Iowa

Finally, a home for the china

This china cabinet project actually got its start during the early 1960s when my then future father-in-law purchased a rose-patterned china set for his wife. After my mother–in-law passed away in 1986, my wife inherited the china. It had been stored in boxes since then and my wife had been bugging me to build a cabinet in which to display her china. In 1996, my daughter and son-in-law built a new home and purchased a china cabinet, so my wife gave the china to them to display. Well, lo and behold, my daughter decided to decorate not with rose patterns, but with a magnolia motif. So, the china got packed away yet again.

About the middle of October 1998, my daughter and her husband began asking when I was going to build a china cabinet. I figured it was about time, so I visited several local furniture stores to see what was available. During these visits I took pictures and jotted down dimensions so that I could have something to work from. I was not that impressed with anything available in the stores. With this is mind, my son-in-law and I decided to start building.

He first wanted to know what size I planned to make it. I looked at my daughter's cabinet, and then at the pictures I had taken of the retail models. While I was trying to figure out a good size, I remembered that I had some glass shelves stashed away that had been given to me some years ago. I dug them out. They measured 60 in. long and 14 in. deep. I surely didn't want to cut them down, so we went with that length for the cabinet width and the project was underway.

Because of other commitments, we could only work Monday and Friday evenings and Saturday afternoons (when the Arkansas Razorbacks weren't playing football), as I had to cut and deliver firewood in the morning. Eventually, it got to be early November, and the project had to be completed by Christmas. I purchased the lumber (solid oak and oak-grained plywood), and we started the task of building. Everything went rather smoothly for the shelving case, and the top cap was completed in a very short time.

Next came the base cabinet component. We cut and glued up the face frame. The next day, I saw a design I liked better on the Internet and decided to change the front facing to have one large door on either side and four drawers down the center. The others were skeptical about wanting to make a change with the frame already glued up. Needless to say, I prevailed.

From there, everything went very well. I stained it on December 13th, a professional painter applied the lacquer, and it was ready for Christmas. When my wife first saw it on Christmas Eve she was speechless. She had surmised what the "project" might be, but had not sensed how big and beautiful it would turn out. We are all very proud of this project and will be for years to come.

Barry Comer
Jacksonville, Arkansas

Shop-made entertainment centers outlive the competition

The total material cost to build both of these entertainment centers was still just a fraction in comparison to store-bought models. And the factory-made pieces I've found warp severely with just a small amount of moisture in the air inside a home. After investing in several of these flawed entertainment centers and being disappointed every time, I decided to take a different approach. I built my own, and it worked. It made my wife happy and now I am happy too. Since last year, I've put five of these entertainment centers together!

David Martinez
Shamrock, Texas

Bench is a wheel of a project

An antique benchboard seat at a friend's house inspired this woodworking project. The legs are constructed of two pieces of ¾-in. plywood glued together and cut in the shape of an arc. The spindles are actually long, slender wooden octagons. I carved a starburst into both sides. The hub was turned on the lathe and quartered. I built the remainder of the seat from ¾-in. pine. It's a very roomy piece to sit in, and the quarter-wagon wheel look gives it a pleasing antique appearance.

Quint Bennett
Franklin Grove, Illinois

Headboard to backrest

What to do with discarded headboards? That's what I wondered when my wife brought home a twin-size headboard from the furniture store where she worked part-time. They were going to throw it out since it was an oddball piece. I decided to make this bench out of it. I bought some bed rail brackets (from the same furniture store), attached them to the bench part that I had made from the same type of wood and stained to match the headboard. Voila! A new family room bench was created. This is an inexpensive way to add a new piece of furniture to your home while recycling parts that would normally just be thrown out.

John Ziemba
Denver, Pennsylvania

No need to pine
for this bedroom set

This was my woodworking project for
1999: A full bedroom set with chest,
dresser, headboard and footboard. The
bed rails, although not visible in the
photos, are white pine 1 × 6s with angle
iron fastened to the backs. I wanted the
headboard raised 2 in. off the floor to
see the side rail. To accomplish this,
I made the side rail with a 5° bevel on
each end so the head and footboard
would sit straight up. The dresser,
chest and sides, along with the headboard and footboards, have white
pine inserts with small grooves
cut equally from side to side. The
framing is also white pine.

Carl Hucks
Georgetown, South Carolina

Accessories

Boxes full of history

For over seventy-five years the majestic Moreton Bay Fig tree stood on the property line between the Thomas Edison and Henry Ford summer estates in Fort Myers, Florida. The huge tree, with above ground roots rising over 7 ft. in some places, had been a popular site ever since the estates were opened to the public in 1947.

Unfortunately, high winds caused an 8-ton limb to come crashing from the tree in 1994. For safety reasons, the entire fig had to be removed. I visited the site the morning after the storm. It was a shame to see such a historically significant natural wonder being dismantled by chainsaws and hauled to the dump grounds. I had to do something to preserve the tree's memory.

Eventually, after some talking, I convinced the officials at the estate to give me some of the wood so I could come up with a keepsake project. I designed and began making these small boxes. Now, the Edison-Ford Estate sells them in its gift shop. I have sold over 900 boxes made from the wood of the Moreton Bay Fig tree that Thomas Edison planted almost 80 years ago.

William Thorne
Fort Myers, Florida

Thomas Alva Edison's Moreton Bay Fig
Edison - Ford Winter Estate Fort Myers, Florida

Photo courtesy of Edison-Ford Winter Estate

Cradling a family's past with wood

I have made nine cradles in this design, all for my grandchildren. Four of these have been crafted in the last eight years, while I've been confined to a wheelchair. My family helped set up my shop to accommodate the wheelchair and my woodworking hasn't skipped a beat! This past winter, I finished my latest cradle in time for the birth of my first great-grandchild. The material for each is solid cherry. One panel of every cradle I've made comes from a 38-ft. cherry tree that blew down in our yard from a tornado 15 years ago. That tree was

very popular with my eight children, who used to swing from it and play under its shade while growing up. Instead of hauling the limbs and trunk to the dump, I had the wood milled into boards. Because I want to include a piece of this history in any future cradles I might make, I only include a small amount of this special cherry in each project. The cradles have been a big hit with all my children, grandchildren and now great-grandchildren. The family cat even used one to have her litter of kittens!

Paul Zajac
Gibsonia, Pennsylvania

Radiator cover-up scandalous for dust

Here's a simple project I built to replace inefficient radiator covers. Even though my mother was a meticulous house cleaner, I never once saw her remove the radiator covers in order to clean behind them. This is a popular spot for dust to gather, making the radiator less effective at heating the house. Also, most covers don't allow the air to circulate very well. My model is much more efficient when it comes to air circulation. I built a vent right into the ceramic tile top. Since the top is just a single tile thick, most of the radiator is exposed, making it much easier to clean around.

Timothy McIntyre
Saint Louis, Missouri

Tuck-away design keeps stool a step ahead

This step stool with a tuck-away step is constructed of oak. The joinery is mortise-and-tenon. I cut a ¾-in. dado to make the track for the pullout step. In the middle of the step, I put a dowel to act as a stop and keep the lower step from pulling out on its own. There's a 5⁄16-in. dado toward the front and another toward the back, where a 2-in. filler block keeps the step from pulling out. I centered a hole on the top for carrying the stool. All the edges were rounded over with my router. It has a golden oak stain and three coats of polyurethane.

Robert Lopes
North Dighton, Massachusetts

"Model" citizen fashions childhood tractor from wood

I have made presents for all the kids in the family for years. One year, I made one little boy a tractor and trailer out of wood. I wrote on the trailer "You Call, We Haul," and wrote his name and phone number below it. That was a big hit.

My dad farmed until I was eight years old. This came to mind when I needed another gift one Christmas. I made a model International Harvester McCormick Farmall tractor from wood, because that was the machine my dad used in his fields. This project was also an entry in the county fair woodworking contest. It has all the same parts as a real McCormick Farmall, and they're all in the proper places. It's made mostly out of pine, but the axle pins and wheels are made of oak. I even wired the "engine" with telephone wire.

I used an old child's toy tractor to get the size right. I used my memory to approximate the shape and position of the parts. Books from the library were also a big help.

John Bring
Thief River Falls, Minnesota

Multi-task table solves workshop dilemma

I had a storage and space problem in my new workshop. I retired just three years ago and built my retirement dream of a 10 × 20-ft. wood shop attached to my carport. My mistake was not making it large enough to accommodate all my woodworking tools. I am constantly moving work stations around to create more space. I needed a piece that would do multiple functions. After several attempts, I came up with this solution that solved my problem.

This is the mobile workstation that I designed to solve my dilemma. Made of Philippine mahogany, the cabinet houses my table saw, allowing me to cut full sheets of plywood with ease. I can clamp a fence on either side to cut pieces wider than the saw table allows. It contains five drawers, two doors and one open storage area for all my optional accessories. I added lockable casters for easy movement. It includes a removable top, which allows me to attach portable power tools like a drill press and band saw. It also serves as a workbench, providing the flexibility I need in my cramped shop. Also incorporated is a vacuum hose opening in the rear for use with the table saw.

Raymond Beauchemin
Mililani, Hawaii

Member puts his heart into girlfriend's step stool

This is one of my wood shop projects. It's a stool fashioned from 1-in. oak. This design is one of the most durable stools I've ever made, and can easily withstand the weight of any full-grown man. For a little extra flair, I inlaid a heart, along with my girlfriend's initial, into the oak. I used a couple of coats of wipe-on polyurethane for the finish. As you can see, this stool is simple to construct, requiring only a couple of screws and some glue to assemble.

Richard Derengowski
Chicago, Illinois

Projects drive home joy of woodworking

Here are a couple of my favorite woodworking projects. The model semi-truck is one of several I made for my co-workers when I was a truck driver for Bush's Canned Foods. Each truck is 40-42 in. long. They come in two parts—the cab and the trailer—that connect at the fifth wheel. I used white pine for the material, and hand-painted the markings. It took about 2-3 weeks to complete one truck. The bird feeder is a design I've sold several of through the years. These two projects are just a couple of my woodworking successes. As you can see, I love spending time in the wood shop.

Everette Grigsby
Del Rio, Tennessee

Drawers, drawers and more drawers!

I made this 190-drawered storage cabinet for use in my shop. It's helpful for organizing fasteners and other small pieces of hardware, along with drill and router bits. I made the cabinet from scrap birch I got from the trailer shop where I worked in Syracuse, Indiana. Each side has drawers. The drawers vary in width. One side has one 12-in. drawer at each row, one has two 6-in. drawers, one has three 4-inchers and one side has four 3-in. drawers. I set the unit on a lazy Susan base to make the drawers easier to get at. I also installed skate wheels to make the cabinet mobile.

Even though I love woodworking, I never imagined how boring it could be to cut the drawer parts all day long. There were piles of parts all over my garage. I used dado and rabbet joints on each drawer. My wife helped me put them together with a nail gun. After filling all the nailholes, I hand-dipped each drawer into a container of wood sealer to make sure that the seal coat covered every surface (it was also less tedious than brushing it on). I made a jig to position all the drawer pulls consistently. The pulls are nothing more than inexpensive conduit clamps.

Jim Kuhl
Elmira, New York

Hunting for a gift idea

When my sister asked me if I could build a gun cabinet for her husband, who is a big time hunting and fishing nut, I said I would be happy to. She presented me with a picture of a cabinet that he indicated was just what he was looking for. Without measurements or details to go by, I drew out plans and began putting it together. I used oak and oak veneer, for the most part. I also made the handles out of deer antlers, which I had in my shop. All in all, he was very surprised when my sister presented it to him for Christmas last year. Happy hunting, Dan!

Anthony Jandreau
Fort Kent, Maine

Country cart handy around the yard

This mobile garden tool holder is a handy helper around the house. The four casters on the bottom allow me to wheel it to wherever I happen to be working in the yard or garden. The lattice panels in the top and bottom act as holders for the handles of various tools. The frame is painted with my original country decorations.

William Tito
Milwaukee, Wisconsin

Model engine delivers mail to member's door

Here's my steam engine mailbox woodworking project. The mailbox is modeled after the Union Pacific 4-4-0 and is made out of a standard black mailbox, pine lumber, a craft bell, two wire coat hangers and three colors of paint. There are two sets of wheels—two large wheels in the back and two small wheels in the front. All of the wheels move. It's possible to reach inside the cab and ring the bell located just in front of the smokestack. The bell is attached with fishing line secured in the cab with a screw. The handrails that are found running down both sides of the boiler are made out of wire coat hangers. Finally, my family name, preceded by the number one, is painted on both sides of the cab. There is another white "1" painted on the nose.

Frank Tietjen III
Ulster Park, New York

Table scraps

I built this 48 × 28 × 20-in. rolling tool cabinet/shop side table completely out of recycled materials. The lumber I used consisted of scrap wood left over from our new home, which was built in 1998. The species are pine, cherry and oak. The bumpers on the bottom are scrap oak handrails typically used for staircases. The brass handles were recycled from old windows, replaced before selling our previous home. I just love having the ability to wheel my tools around the shop.

Mike Wozniczka
Farmington, Minnesota

Manufacturers can't hold a candle to these homemade holders

Working with wood is the joy of my retired life. As a woodworker I design wood projects that people want. A challenge I took on recently was to design candleholders for a church in Rocklin, California.

No commercial candleholder fit the church's needs. The requirements were to design a holder that could be secured to the pews and removed without damaging the finish on the pews. Burning candles presented a fire safety issue. Candle wax on the carpet was another issue. Any candleholder must absorb a bump without being dislodged. The holders had to accept long candles within a chimney, as well as shorter candles in crystal holders. The holders are used as bases when decorating for special occasions in the church, such as weddings. The holders had to be easily removed from the pews and stored.

My design met all the church's requirements. The holders are designed to clamp onto the top of the pew. No connecting pegs or screws are visible. The slider assembly that allows for easy removal of the holders is attached with a cap screw, which threads into a well nut screwed into the rear block between the two side rails. The rails are pegged to the top. To attach the holder, a ¼-in. ratchet with a hex head is inserted and very gently the slide mechanism slides against the pew, pulling the back forward and pinching the holder in place. It's a very simple operation for the elderly ladies who prepare the church for special services. The holder does not mark the finish of the pew at all. I proudly constructed a total of 20 holders. It is a joy to see my craftsmanship put to such a good cause in the community.

David Wickstrom
Roseville, California

A more efficient router table base on wheels

I was not happy with my router table, so I sold it! However, the base on my new model wasted a lot of space, which was not a good thing in my basement shop. With the help of TurboCAD computer software, I drew up several designs for a new, more space-efficient router table. This is what I came up with.

The new router table cabinet has abundant usability. It is built with mahogany plywood, trimmed with white oak and finished with oil-based stain and clear polyurethane. I decided to expose the locking swivel castors by mounting them on ¾-in. solid oak and arcing the toe kick plate to add a touch of style.

The two bottom drawers on this case are mounted on full-extension drawer slides with nickel handles. They are useful to store routers, jigs, templates and fences. The four upper drawers are simply "wood on wood" drawers (no slides). They contain router bit holders, as well as miscellaneous tools.

A space for the vacuum makes this cabinet a true winner. The door is held closed with two brass double ball catches, eliminating vacuum noise. In the back

of the cabinet, the hose has a hole to access the fence on the router table. The two other holes are for the power cord and to provide airflow from the vacuum.

The router table has a 3.5 hp, variable speed plunge router mounted under it. It also has a central power switch to turn on the router and the vacuum at the same time. This can all be quickly removed by loosening the four wing nuts so that other tools, such as a spindle sander, can be set in place.

After working with several designs, I believe that I made the right choice. I learned many new techniques while building something I will cherish for many years. I am very proud of my router table cabinet set-up.

Glen Kadlebach
Hutchinson, Minnesota

Backyard

A new angle on deck building

I have built a few decks in the past for friends and neighbors. These were always just the plain old rectangular shape. When I bought my house, I wanted to do something different. I designed and built this pressure-treated deck/gazebo that is 21 × 14 ft. with an 8-sided, 12-ft. gazebo attached to one corner. The decking runs in a diagonal pattern towards the gazebo, with the gazebo in an octagonal pattern. It took me about two months working weekends and evenings to complete the project. One piece of advice for anyone planning to build a gazebo—practice cutting 22½° angles!

Lawrence Kelly
Havre de Grace, Maryland

This deck's a wrap

This deck and backyard pond are newly completed as of last summer. I needed a large deck to wrap around my new addition, and to make use of all the new French doors I installed. I wanted a unique deck. That's why I chose this rounded style with an 11-ft. radius, and used copper for the rails and balusters rather than the traditional wood. These rails and balusters are nothing more than ¾-in. copper pipe which I polished and coated with clear enamel. I enclosed the bottom with matching cedar lattice and put up a short wall of interlocking blocks. Between them, I filled in wood chips and planted a few bushes. I built up a flagstone pond off the front of the deck. There's a small fountain jet that shoots water into the air, producing a very relaxing sound while we are enjoying the peace and quiet of our new little backyard retreat. The final step in the entire project was the brick landing and walkway between the deck and the garage. I've never seen a deck quite like this one, and I'm very proud of its unique design.

Ernie Reilly
Reno, Nevada

The generous curve in the design (above) provides a natural place for a stylish rounded patio table and chairs set that clutters up the middle of most square or rectangular decks. The sleek copper balusters open up sightlines so often obscured by traditional wooden railings.

Ernie's arcing deck design (above) makes particularly good use of his twin sets of French doors which open directly onto the handsomely landscaped backyard.

To top it all off, Ernie added a flagstone pond jutting out from his wrap-around deck (left). The pond eases a slight dip in the yard, and acts as a transition between the higher ground and the lower. A small fountain jet completes the project.

The envy of handymen everywhere

This is a picture of my shop I've been working on for the last few years. I have done everything myself, except pour the concrete floor and taping/texturing the interior walls. The shop is 24 × 40 ft. The back half is set up for woodworking, and the front half is for working on cars. The first 20-ft. section has 10-ft. ceilings with easily accessible storage above the overhead door. The last 20-ft. half of the building has a vaulted 12 ft., 8-in. ceiling that is nice for flipping large projects around in. The inside walls and ceilings are all finished with wallboard, textured and painted white so it is nice and bright to work in. On the outside front of the shop, I continued the brickwork already on the house. I have also matched the siding, trim, windows and roof so the house and the shop look made for each other.

I installed a 100,000 BTU propane furnace at the peak of the far end with lots of insulation in the walls and ceilings so it warms up fast and stays toasty during cold Idaho winters. The walls are all piped with compressed air that I have plumbed outside underground to a garden shed that houses the compressor. I have 100-amp service running into the shop, so I can run just about anything I need to. To make it easy to get equipment and materials in and out, I installed a 9 × 16-ft. overhead garage door. This is an ongoing project that has been a lot of fun. It is nice to finally have enough room to work on all my projects.

Delane Anderson
Chubbuck, Idaho

Rocky project halts erosion

I was having trouble with run-off from my barn roof—too much roof and no gutters! Gutters would not have handled the bulk of water coming of the roof. I decided to do the next best thing to protect the ground from erosion. The ground along the 60-ft. front porch had a natural slope where the water had been running. I had to fill in a lot of ruts so I decided to put in more fill, and raise a bed to plant shrubs and some other vegetation in. Next, I had to determine how far out from the building the water would flow off the roof. I then cut a sloping trench the length of the building. Covering this with plastic, I then ran a garden hose over the plastic. This made a natural slope at one end where I dug a catch basin connected to drain pipe running to the pond below. This seems to be enough to handle the amount of water. Next, I arranged flat flagstone along the sides of the trench. This created a splash block to help disperse the water onto the mound, plants and yard. Although it felt as if I moved tons of stone for this project, it seems to all have been worthwhile.

Richard Drake
Greenfield, Indiana

One swingin' outdoor design

This is my trellis-swing combination. I built it entirely out of cedar. The swing is 4-ft. wide. The arch is made of six pieces cut at 15° angles, then half-lapped together. The 1-in. deck lumber and 2 × 6-in. board ripped in half create a very sturdy frame for the swing. The curve of the seat and the back make it quite comfortable to sit in.

Todd Gibb
Saint Anne, Illinois

Stairway to storage

This is my stairway-shed project. By enclosing the "dead" space below the stairs up to my back deck I was able to create valuable, usable space without adding on additional footage (and therefore additional taxes). It was easy to construct because all the heavy framing work was already done. Since there were no structural changes made, no expensive building permits were needed and I didn't have to delay construction to schedule an inspector. There was no digging necessary because the base is attached above ground only. I was happy to not have to shingle the roof. This style shed blends right in with my house and its surroundings while an out building tends to clutter the property it sits on. Also, this storage shed can't get much closer to the house.

Bernard Hoffman
Hawley, Pennsylvania

The Empire strikes back

I built this "Empire Deck and Patio Cover" out of heart redwood. The entire project is my design, including the rafter tails and privacy screen pickets. There is a storage box next to the barbecue grill for charcoal and other materials. A planter box along the steps acts as a safety rail. There's a bench seat following the contour of the windbreak wall on the inside. The top of the windbreak wall is angled as it approaches the steps to provide a handrail. At night, I turn on the recessed rope lighting to provide a soft glow throughout the deck area. To free up some of my garage space, I attached a small shed where I can store my lawnmower and other maintenance items. The appliques on the upright posts provide a clue as to where the name of the project originated. The geometric Art Deco motif is a tribute to the Empire State Building in New York City. I, too, come from the Empire State originally.

Jim Brown
Reno, Nevada

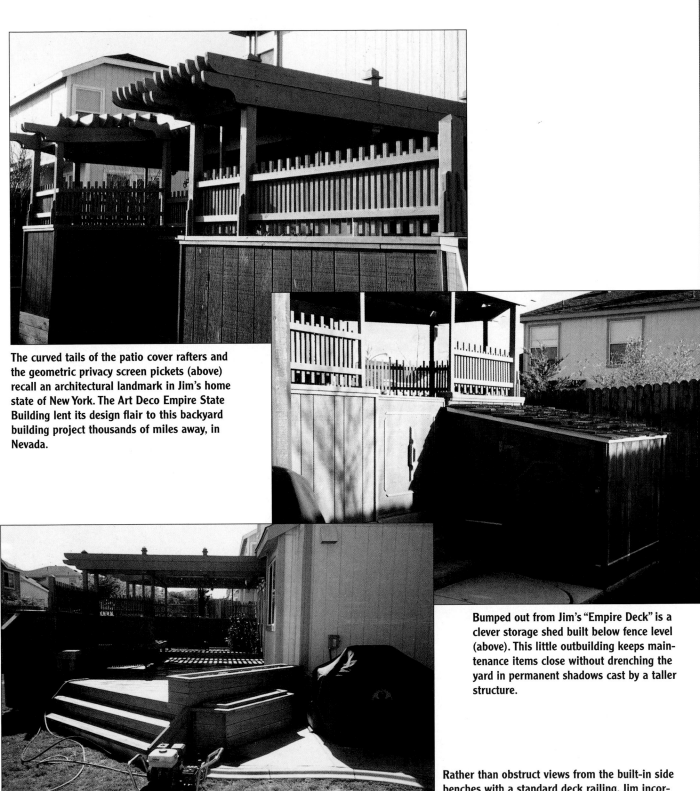

The curved tails of the patio cover rafters and the geometric privacy screen pickets (above) recall an architectural landmark in Jim's home state of New York. The Art Deco Empire State Building lent its design flair to this backyard building project thousands of miles away, in Nevada.

Bumped out from Jim's "Empire Deck" is a clever storage shed built below fence level (above). This little outbuilding keeps maintenance items close without drenching the yard in permanent shadows cast by a taller structure.

Rather than obstruct views from the built-in side benches with a standard deck railing, Jim incorporated a planter box to double as a safety feature (left). Below the planter is another covered box that contains Jim's grilling supplies.

Royally fun kids project

I built this scrap-wood castle for my grandchildren. Inside on the bottom floor is a large play area and a ladder that leads to the upper lookout towers. On the backside of the castle there is a slide for the kids to go down. The overhang provides a top and shade for the sandbox. After it was completed, my wife and I painted the castle gray and then used a sponge to give it the look of a brick exterior. The kids love it!

Gary Hall
Linden, Michigan

Elevated deck doesn't leak on lower level

I wanted to build an elevated deck out from the new French doors in my family room. The deck would be right above the entrance to the walkout guest quarters. I did not want rainwater, snowmelt or spillage to leak down through the deck planking onto the entrance and patio below.

I designed and constructed a deck to solve my dilemma. This deck is entirely maintenance free. It is supported by 36-in. deep, 24 × 24-in footings upon which I mounted 10-in. fiberglass-reinforced polymer columns. These columns, in turn, support a crossbeam made up of three 2 × 8-in. boards spiked and bolted together. The deck joists are also 2 × 8s. In between the joists, granular-surfaced roll roofing creates a "roof" to prevent anything from spilling through. The roofing is supported on ½-in. exterior plywood, which is sloped toward the outer edge of the deck where the water drains into a plastic eave and to a downspout. Synthetic planks were used for the decking and vinyl posts and rails for the railings. The rim and face joists are covered with baked-enamel aluminum sheeting, which I had bent to my specifications at a reasonable cost.

I obtained a building permit from the local authority. At the final inspection the inspector wrote, "Great Job!" on the permit. He told me that the design and craftsmanship were better than nine out of 10 contractors could have done.

Frederick Wright
Provo, Utah

Shop-made gazebo kit really delivers

When I returned to New York from New Mexico after recovering from a hcart attack, my brother asked me to design and build him a gazebo. I produced an entire set of plans and specs for the project. Since I assumed that a gazebo 8 ft. or smaller would be more decorative than useful, I made one with a 12 ft diameter. Since a transport permit is required to deliver anything over 8 ft. in width, I designed one in a kit form with two floor sections that were bolted together on-site. Each side panel was made in a jig to make sure that all eight were the same. The angle braces and latticework were left out on the entrance section. This "kit" allowed the gazebo to be placed where a fully assembled one could not be delivered.

Robert Shrauger
Marathon, New York

Lidded sandbox keeps cats away, lets children play

I recently completed this sandbox project for my grandchildren. My son wanted a lid for the huge sandbox for two reasons: First, to keep the neighborhood cats from using it as a litter box, and second so the kids could leave their toys in it when not playing there. I decided on a 7 × 7-ft. sandbox. I purchased all the materials (exterior plywood, screws, paint, moisture-resistant wood glue, etc.). Everything is glued and screwed together. I sanded both the inside and the outside very thoroughly to reduce the risk of splinters. I used the leftover pieces of plywood to make a seat in each corner of the sandbox.

Since the lid would have been too heavy for my daughter-in-law to lift, I made it in two sections with an overlapping joint in the center. Each section is attached to the rear of the box with 8-in. gate hinges. Each lid section has a handle to make opening and closing it a little easier. There's also a 6-in. safety gate hook to secure the lid to the bottom and prevent the children from trying to open the sandbox themselves. When the lid is open, it lays back onto the lawn. Anyone caught playing on top of the lid loses his sandbox privileges. So far, this method of enforcement has worked. It's a pleasure to watch the grandchildren play in the sandbox with their friends. It makes it well worth the time and effort it took to build it.

Vern Pereira
Cumberland, Rhode Island

Space for dad, daughter and dog

This is a two-story shed/clubhouse I built. The top half is a clubhouse with a deck where my daughter can play. The ladder runs down on the outside of my dog's pen so she won't let the dog out every time she wants to use her playhouse. The bottom half is a storage shed, with another deck where my dog can lay and soak up the sun.

Dixon Lougheed, Jr.
Rochester, New York

Oriental bridgework

Here's our Japanese-style curved bridge that spans a stream between two backyard ponds. The bridge is 30 in. wide and 6 ft. long with a rise of 12 in. in the center. In addition, the peak of the rise is offset 15° from center to give it more interest and to allow proper placement between large boulders. I constructed the bridge entirely of recycled 2 × 6-in. redwood deck boards.

Ron Karlic
Orland Park, Illinois

Playing with a full deck after addition

When we purchased our home it did not have a full back deck. We had to climb a steep hill just to reach the existing deck. One of the first home improvement projects I tackled was this full deck addition. It measures approximately 12 × 18 ft. I made it entirely out of pressure-treated lumber. I drew up my own sketches, altered the dimensions as necessary, poured piers, set footings, laid plastic and covered it with crushed rock and then started framing. I used stainless steel angle pieces at all the joist and pole locations to make it stronger. I attached all the decking with screws. Then I added railings to the posts that were already in place, followed by the lattice. To top it all off I connected the stairs, which I had built first in order to make climbing the hill up to the deck much easier. I finished up with some landscaping—added wood chips, built a nice walkway to the deck stairs and seeded in new grass. This project sure adds a lot to the backyard.

Richard Drake
Greenfield, Indiana

After purchasing his new house, Richard decided to make his sloped backyard more usable by adding a walk-out deck with stairs down to the yard. In the photo above, the footings and railing posts have been set.

Richard designed his deck to extend past the corner of the house to tie into a small flower bed landscaped with wood chips that is also home to the central air conditioning unit (above).

A set of stairs extending from the deck to the lower backyard eases the trek up and down the steep slope leading to the house (left). Lattice nailed under the stair treads conceals the rock and plastic spread below the stairs to control the growth of any vegetation.

Remodeling

No more windy sunsets

When my wife and I had our house built we added a covered patio onto the west side so we could enjoy watching the setting sun over the mountains. Thanks to the prevailing westerly winds, however, we soon found out that this dream was not going to be a reality. We then decided to create a porch by enclosing the patio with windows.

We installed patio sliding doors on each end, and sliding windows in front. All this glass gives us good views in three directions, but still keeps the winds out. The area above the windows is filled with ¼-in. plate glass, and the knee wall below the windows is painted white to match the rest of the interior of the house. Mini-blinds are used to control exposure to the sun. This remodel has turned the former patio into a sunroom that can be used nearly year-round. It was a very enjoyable summer project for my wife and me.

Albert Siewert
Helena, Montana

AFTER

BEFORE

"Plain Jane" turns to stone

The fireplace in my home was added after the house was built, and it wasn't to code since the hearth was only 12-in. deep instead of the required 16 in. I had an idea on how to bring the 1978 fireplace up to code and give it a facelift in the process. I wanted to use some 12 × 12-in. red oak timbers I had laying around the yard. Weathered and going to waste, I decided they would be an excellent choice for a rustic mantle. Seeing cultured stone at a local home and garden show gave me further ideas for the facelift. The wheels were turning, so I went for it.

Taking the mantle off of the plain 70s fireplace gave me a clean palette to work with. After some rewiring for new lights and outlets, I set the hearthstones in place. Now I could determine the size of each timber for holding up the mantle. I was not about to haul those 220-pound timbers in and out of the house. Measuring once, twice, three, even four times, then cutting with a chainsaw was the idea. It worked. Then I wondered, "How am I going to get these timbers in place without destroying the hearth

and/or my back?" A light bulb went on: I returned to the garage and dragged my 3-ton hydraulic jack into the living room. My girlfriend just stood there shaking her head saying, "Now what are you going to do with that?"

With the help of my neighbors (who I had bought a case of beer in return for their assistance) I guided the timber into the house on my heavy-duty dolly and slid it onto the jack. I asked my girl-friend to start jacking the timber up above the hearthstone. With me balancing the timber and her jacking it up, we got the timber close. Wrapping my arms around the timber in a bear hug and one loud roar, I lifted and turned it into position. There really was a method to my madness.

I had one more dilemma: Since the cultured stone wasn't going to work on the 2 ¼-in. wide brick face in the vent above the firebox, I went to the tile store to find an alternative. Digging around in some boxes, I found a gold mine! There were exactly 13 tiles in the style I liked, and that was just how many I needed. But 11 of the tiles had to be cut in order to work. I put a concrete cutting blade in my table saw and slowly worked through the stack of tiles. Good luck and patience eventually got me to the point of tiling this one-time "Plain Jane" fireplace.

Next came the cultured stone. After a couple of tries, I got the design I wanted above the mantle. I thought that a big sunburst out of stone would put a bit of artistic flair into this stone collage. After I got all the cultured stone in place, it was time for a break. Eventually, I got to the finishing touches. I stained all the woodwork golden oak and applied a matte finish to the stone. This acts as a protective coat, as well as brings out the color of the stone. It's a natural "wet" look that also makes dusting and cleaning a lot easier. We have had nothing but compliments and praise for the hearth that makes this house a home.

James Madsen
Potterville, Michigan

If you can't find it, build it

The best project that I ever completed was this remodel of my home office. I had two unfinished wood file cabinets that I was waiting to finish until I found a desk that I wanted. Then, after pricing desks and shelves, and not really finding anything I wanted within my budget, I decided to build what I wanted myself. I'm VERY happy that I made this decision.

I didn't want to waste the file cabinets I already owned, so I built these two pieces into the actual shelving. The main framing is strictly 2 × 4s, which I covered in wallboard. I bullnosed all the edges, textured and painted all the parts. I finished the exposed wood, including the shelf caps, the desktop and the file cabinet fronts, with red oak stain. I chose a dark, shiny brass handle for the drawers.

The first step in construction was to pull up the carpet in the room so I could anchor the shelves directly to the concrete slab. Convincing my wife that I needed to rip up the two-year old carpet was quite a hurdle to cross. After that, the framing began by dropping a soffit from the

ceiling on two walls. Next followed the electrical, the drywall and all the finishing. Matching the texture to the existing wall was probably the trickiest part of the whole project.

The best part of this project, besides the money savings, was that I got exactly what I needed: a bunch of shelf space for my junk, a secret hiding place built into a vertical support, a cubby-hole for my computer tower (getting it off the floor), lights just where I needed them, and the satisfaction of a job well done (not to mention the joy of hearing people compliment on how nice it looks).

Ted Wilber
Phoenix, Arizona

Stepping up appearance with deck boards

After tearing up indoor/outdoor carpet on my back steps, the brick was littered with unsightly glue that was difficult to remove. In addition, some pieces of brick were missing altogether. I decided to cover my steps with pressure-treated deck boards attached to the brick with self-tapping concrete anchor screws. Then I painted them with porch and deck enamel. I liked the look of the steps so well that I decided to cover my concrete front porch floor with pressure-treated decking also. For an accent, I built a railing from scrap 2 × 4s, which I ripped to form the balusters and then painted. The only new wood I had to purchase was for the top of the railing. This was a very inexpensive, yet satisfying project!

Robert Strickland
North Charleston, South Carolina

BEFORE

AFTER

Fireplace facelift warms without a flame

My project was to take old unusable fireplaces and turn them into something that brightens up our home. My house is 100 years old and the fireplaces have been painted over at least 20 times through the years. I stripped them down as far as I could, then sanded them smooth. I did the same thing to the floor. I then stained one of the fireplaces to match the floor, and painted the other to match the wall. I painted the metal frameworks of both gold. I built wooden boxes for the broken down interior, creating a shadow box. I then painted the interiors and all the cement work with a faux stone finish. I painted the trim of one royal blue then sat a royal blue vase full of blue flowers in the box I had created. This fireplace now sits in a bedroom. The second one is in the living room. I am 61 years old and this is the biggest project of this sort I have ever tried to do. I am very proud of the outcome.

Bunny Chaney
Abbeville, South Carolina

Old stove gets a new lease on life

I did some remodeling on an old home. On the porch was a rusty Franklin stove. These stoves are made just like a fireplace insert, except they have three legs and are freestanding like a stove. The owner gave it to me and it sat in my shop for a year. I bought a gas log on sale and installed it in the firebox. First, I dismantled the stove and cleaned off all the rust. Then I put the stove backing on all the parts and reassembled the stove. I removed the 8-in. chimney pipe from the top and, since the stove had a conversion panel on the back, I put that on the top instead. In place of the back panel I made a 4-in. steel cover with a 4-in. adapter outlet for a vent (even though the gas log did not require a vent, I included one just in case I want to further modify the stove in the future). In the 4-in. vent pipe I made a damper out of a paint can lid and a piece of stiff wire. With the damper shut, the stove is nearly 100% efficient and the cast iron radiates heat long after the gas log is shut off. Not only does my new stove keep my home warm, it also keeps my coffee cup hot if I set it down on the top while reading my *HANDY* magazine.

Robert Shrauger
Marathon, New York

BEFORE

Whole house overhaul

With the exception of some rough framing and work in the basement, my wife and I have done over 90% of the work on our remodeled home. When I purchased the house it was small, in need of a lot of work, but no big deal to me. I was young, not married and had lots of time on my hands. As time went on, all that changed—a wife, a son, then another on the way. We had to build on to meet our needs. We had to make our house bigger and better.

When we started we had a 900-sq. ft. house with one bathroom, a living room and a kitchen. On the main floor, we had one 8 × 8-ft. bedroom, and a second 13 × 13-ft. bedroom upstairs. There were no closets and the kitchen cabinets were metal. It was a real nightmare of a house. I'm still surprised my wife agreed to move in.

After the remodel, we have over 1600-sq. ft. of space, including three bedrooms (each with its own walk-in closet), a walk-in linen closet and a full upstairs bath. The main floor has a large living area with fireplace, a formal dining room and a ¾ bath. The kitchen is eat-in with a center island. It has solid oak cabinetry and an extra big pantry. A new rear entry room is the perfect place

BEFORE

to take off muddy shoes, and its closet is great for coats, hats, gloves, etc. The entire home is trimmed in oak. It has carpeting throughout except in the entrances, the kitchen and the bathrooms. The wall treatments are a mix of texture and wallpaper.

Although the basement is not finished, we did have rough plumbing installed just in case we decide to finish it. We insulated it to make it warmer in winter and cooler in summer. We also raised the entire house 12 in. when we did the basement. Another added benefit has been the addition of the vertical door into the basement—no more having to shovel snow off the bulkhead to use the outside entrance to the basement.

My wife and I have worked hard on our home. All the hours of ripping out plaster, lath and flooring, as well as running new wiring and flooring have really paid off. We learned valuable lessons installing insulation, hanging sheet rock, taping, texturing and painting. Perhaps the most valuable lesson learned was to not live in the house while such a large project is underway!

Fritz Gaul
Le Mars, Iowa

Satisfaction guaranteed for custom cabinet recipients

After working briefly in a Florida cabinet shop in 1992, I became a stay-at-home mom again. I needed something to do with my time after the daily chores were completed. In the past, I had done small woodworking projects with my husband, and I really enjoyed them. So I decided I would "play" again with the tools and wood.

I had seen the saws and routers in use often, but always in another's hands. It was now time to learn about them firsthand. As you might expect, it has paid off. At first, I tried to make things that were different from what other local folks were making. Many of the projects I did early on were shadow boxes with woodburned scenes mounted to the top of the boxes.

I sold quite a few of those boxes (with many being special orders). People began asking if I could build other things, including mantels and gun cabinets. I was more than happy to build whatever they asked for. I also did some cabinet refacing. The best part of every job was knowing that my customers were satisfied. Of course, the money helped too.

One of my biggest rewards was in the spring of 1993 when I met a woman who wanted me to build cabinets to put in a house she was renovating for her daughter. I built the cabinets from the floor up in the kitchen, and also fashioned a vanity for the bathroom. Since this was my first big project, I was

a bit nervous. I managed to pass the test with flying colors.

I began the project by finding out what my customer wanted and taking down all the measurements. Then, in order to keep her costs down, we headed to the local salvage yard. There, I was able to pick up the framing lumber, along with the drawers and door fronts. The drawers and door fronts were the same style, but all needed to be stripped so I could apply a matching finish.

My customer picked out the paneling she wanted for the faces of the cabinets, and ordered Formica from a local hardware store. I came across a good deal on a stainless steel sink. After all the materials were assembled, I set out to really put my handy skills to the test.

Once the framing and facing were done, I built drawers to fit. With a lot of sanding and blending, all the doors and drawer fronts matched. My husband helped me with the counter, and when it was time he helped me install the cabinets onto the concrete walls.

The woman and her daughter were both thrilled and totally amazed. I think my husband was pretty astounded too. My customer and I see each other on a regular basis. I've yet to hear any complaints.

Shane Cothern
Blackshear, Georgia

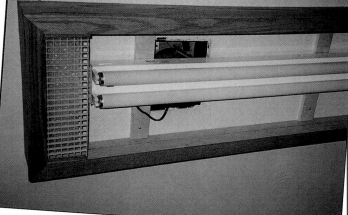

Grate idea for light fixtures

I made this custom wood cover for my bathroom fan/light combination. Not only was it easy and inexpensive to build, but it also greatly improves the appearance of our bathroom. The fluorescent bulbs light the room much better than the last fixture, and the fan still functions thanks to the egg crate louver grates I designed into each end of the cover. The wood grid was made by cutting a series of dadoes into the cross pieces to form lap joints.

Ronald Crawford
Susquehanna, Pennsylvania

Cabinets on the cheap

To keep the costs down during a remodel of the kitchen in my rented apartment, the landlord agreed to let me tackle the work. I made all of the cabinets out of ¾-in. lauan plywood. It worked out great to put a nice finish on them using a graining system I bought at my local home center. This is a convenient way to achieve exactly the look you want, and it's simple too. First apply a base coat of primer and let it dry. Then apply the stain, which needs to sit for a few minutes. Finally, you can use the graining tool to apply whatever grain pattern you want. How's that for "custom cabinets?" I cut corners on cost by buying all of the hardware at a yard sale. The whole bill came in right around $250. Call me cheap? You bet!

Robert Medeiros
South Dartmouth, Massachusetts

AFTER

BEFORE

Crafty patio enclosure creates storage space

Twenty-two years ago we moved from Fairbanks, Alaska, to Ninety Six, South Carolina. Once we arrived, I drew up the plans for our house. Then I hired the excavator, mason, framer, plumber, electrician, finish carpenter, roofer and landscaper to build the home on the two acres of land that we had purchased. For twenty-one years we lived with a patio on the side of our home that we hardly ever used. It's on the southwestern side of the house. Therefore, it's always too hot during the day to sit and enjoy ourselves.

My wife is involved in craft-making—pillows, pot holders, dish towels, hanging baskets, swags, pouting baby dolls, holiday ornaments etc. And I do wood crafts such as vegetable bins, tissue holders and cedar boxes. A year ago, I became aware of a problem. All of the empty space in the house, including the guestroom and all the closets, were full of all the crafts we were making. It was obvious that we needed to do something concerning a place to store all those crafts.

The answer to my problem was found on the rarely used patio. This 14-ft. wide × 50-ft. long space was perfect. Since my wife insisted on keeping a small portion of the patio intact, we only enclosed 42 ft. of the space with windows. We had already put the patio roof on years ago,

so all it took was to frame in the space and install 15 windows. The glass in the windows is reflective, so it looks like a mirror from the outside and has a very handsome bronze appearance. I had originally built a continuous bench along the outside wall of the patio. I decided to leave this bench in position, and it now serves as an ideal place to set things.

The patio walls are secured to the brick walls of the house with anchor bolts. We found indoor-outdoor carpet with a very hard backing, and therefore we did not need to put down an underlayment on the patio floor. After one year, it's still perfect. My wife now uses the space to sell her crafts out of. I thoroughly enjoyed working on this project. My friend said, "Well you have a whole summer project ahead of you." I completed it in just six weeks with the help of a lifelong friend, who came to spend a week with us and found himself put to work nearly everyday.

Floyd Helm
Ninety Six, South Carolina

AFTER

BEFORE

Usable space brought forward in kitchen remodel

This winter, my wife and I replaced the cabinets, countertop and tile floor in our 1960s kitchen. The cabinets required assembly and hanging. The floor is a dog of a job when you're 70 years old. Anyway, the cabinet over the refrigerator was totally useless because of its inaccessibility and because of the stuff placed on top of the fridge. Yet, leaving the cabinet out was no solution.

So I designed and built a box to fit that space, which is joined to a new cabinet in the front. This moved the accessibility of the cabinet to right above the fridge door. Now we have storage space 26 in. deep and 12 in. high, plus a shelf. We keep little used appliances in the back, and more frequently used items up front. Getting into the old cabinet meant finding the kitchen stool/ladder and pushing the clutter off the top of the fridge, but now there's no clutter.

The new cabinet was easy to modify. It came with a horizontally split back. In effect, I didn't even use the bottom half of it. I moved the bottom hanger board in the back upward to coincide with the bottom edge of the soffit, which gave this cabinet something to ride on while I fumbled for screws and a screwdriver. It worked perfectly.

Doug Ploss
Antioch, Illinois

New heater changes what's in store

We had a big storage problem. Specifically, we needed a pantry for food and supplies beyond the basic storage in our kitchen cabinets. Coincidentally, our forced-air heating unit was giving us problems. This unit was located in a closet off the kitchen. I asked a friend of mine who's also a heating expert if he could install a heating/air conditioning unit in the attic of our one-story home. He said he could, and you ought to see the plant he installed! He suspended it from the roof rafters and included a long, over-size return air duct that is virtually silent in our home.

Now for my part. I turned the former heater closet into the most beautiful and practical kitchen companion pantry in town (or so my wife says, anyway). I lowered the floor, patched a lot of holes, installed a 24-in. door that matches our home's other doors, installed a ceiling light and a "U" shaped six level storage shelf system that gives us a mini grocery store right at home. I am a 72-year-old retiree, and found this to be a most rewarding project.

Wilbur Frederick
Camarillo, California

Index